06/12

D0992189

TRAILBLAZERS
IN SCIENCE AND TECHNOLOGY

Alfred Blalock, Helen Taussig & Vivien Thomas

MENDING CHILDREN'S HEARTS

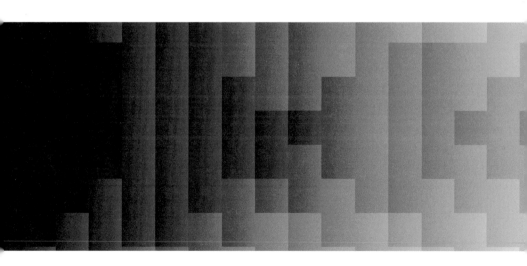

TRAILBLAZERS
IN SCIENCE AND TECHNOLOGY

Alfred Blalock, Helen Taussig & Vivien Thomas

MENDING CHILDREN'S HEARTS

Lisa Yount

CHELSEA HOUSE
An Infobase Learning Company

Alfred Blalock, Helen Taussig, and Vivien Thomas: Mending Children's Hearts
Copyright © 2012 by Lisa Yount

Chelsea House
An imprint of Infobase Learning
132 West 31st Street
New York NY 10001

Library of Congress Cataloging-in-Publication Data

Yount, Lisa.
Alfred Blalock, Helen Taussig, and Vivien Thomas : mending children's hearts / Lisa Yount.
   p. cm.—(Trailblazers in science and technology)
  Includes bibliographical references and index.
  ISBN 978-1-60413-658-6
  1. Blalock, Alfred, 1899–1964. 2. Taussig, Helen B. (Helen Brooke), 1898–1986. 3. Thomas, Vivien T., 1910–1985. 4. Heart surgeons—United States—Biography. 5. Pediatric cardiology—History. I. Title. II. Series.
RD598.Y68 2011
617.4'12092—dc22   [B] 2010035656

Chelsea House books are available at special discounts when purchased in bulk quantities for businesses, associations, institutions, or sales promotions. Please call our Special Sales Department in New York at (212) 967-8800 or (800) 322-8755.

You can find Chelsea House on the World Wide Web at http://www.chelseahouse.com

Excerpts included herewith have been reprinted by permission of the copyright holders; the author has made every effort to contact copyright holders. The publishers will be glad to rectify, in future editions, any errors or omissions brought to their notice.

Text design and composition by Erika K. Arroyo
Illustrations by Bobbi McCutcheon
Photo research by Suzanne M. Tibor
Cover printed by Bang Printing, Brainerd, Minn.
Book printed and bound by Bang Printing, Brainerd, Minn.
Date printed: October 2011
Printed in the United States of America

10 9 8 7 6 5 4 3 2 1

This book is printed on acid-free paper.

To the other members of two trios I am lucky enough to belong to:
Julie and Debbie,
Kat and Verah
— *Love, from the third Wyrd Sister*

Contents

Preface

Trailblazers in Science and Technology is a multivolume set of biographies for young adults that profiles 10 individuals or small groups who were trailblazers in science—in other words, those who made discoveries that greatly broadened human knowledge and sometimes changed society or saved many lives. In addition to describing those discoveries and their effects, the books explore the qualities that made these people trailblazers, the personal relationships they formed, and the way those relationships interacted with their scientific work.

What does it take to be a trailblazer, in science or any other field of human endeavor?

First, a trailblazer must have imagination: the power to envision a path where others see only expanses of jungle, desert, or swamp. Helen Taussig, Alfred Blalock, and Vivien Thomas imagined an operation that could help children whose condition everyone else thought was hopeless. Louis and Mary Leakey looked at shards of bone embedded in the rocks of an African valley and pictured in them the story of humanity's birth.

Imagination alone will not blaze a trail, however. A trailblazer must also have determination and courage, the will to keep on trudging and swinging a metaphorical machete long after others fall by the wayside. Pierre and Marie Curie stirred their witch's cauldron for day after day in a dirty shed, melting down tons of rock to extract a tiny sample of a strange new element. The women astronomers who assisted Edward Pickering patiently counted and compared white spots on thousands of photographs in order to map the universe.

Because their vision is so different from that of others, trailblazers often are not popular. They may find themselves isolated even from those who are working toward the same goals, as Rosalind Franklin did in her research on DNA. Other researchers may brand them as outsiders and therefore ignore their work, as mathematicians did at first with Edward Lorenz's writings on chaos theory because Lorenz's background was in meteorology (weather science), a quite different scientific discipline. Society may regard them as eccentric or worse, as happened to electricity pioneer Nikola Tesla and, to a lesser extent, genome analyst and entrepreneur Craig Venter. This separateness sometimes freed and sometimes hindered these individuals' creative paths.

On the other hand, the relationships that trailblazers do form often sustain them and enrich their work. In addition to supplying emotional and intellectual support, compatible partners of whatever type can build on one another's ideas to achieve insights that neither would have been likely to develop alone. Two married couples described in this set, the Curies and the Leakeys, not only helped each other in their scientific efforts but inspired some of their children to continue on their path. Other partnerships, such as the one between Larry Page and Sergey Brin, the computer scientists-turned-entrepreneurs who founded the Internet giant Google, related strictly to business, but they were just as essential to the partners' success.

Even relationships that have an unhealthy side may prove to offer unexpected benefits. Pickering hired women such as Williamina Fleming to be his astronomical "computers" because he could pay them far less than he would have had to give men for the same work. Similarly, Alfred Blalock took advantage of Vivien Thomas's limited work choices as an African American to keep Thomas at his command in the surgical laboratory. At the same time, these instances of exploitation, so typical of the society of the times, gave the "exploited" opportunities that they would not otherwise have had. Thomas would not have contributed to lifesaving surgeries if he had remained a carpenter in Nashville, even though he might have earned more money than he did by working for Blalock. Fleming surely would never have discovered her talent for astronomy if Pickering had kept her as merely his "Scottish maid."

Competitors can form almost as close a relationship as cooperative partners, and like the irritating grain of sand in an oyster's shell that eventually yields a pearl, rivalries can inspire scientific trailblazers to heights of achievement that they might not have attained if they had worked unopposed. Tesla's competition with Thomas Edison to establish a grid of electrical power around U.S. cities stimulated as well as infuriated both men. Venter's announcement that he would produce a readout of humanity's genes sooner than the massive, government-funded Human Genome Project (HGP) pushed him, as well as his rival, HGP leader Francis Collins, to greater efforts. The French virologist Luc Montagnier was spurred to refine and prove his suspicions about the virus he thought was linked to AIDS because he knew that Robert Gallo, a similar researcher in another country, was close to publishing the same conclusions.

It is our hope that the biographies in the Trailblazers in Science and Technology set will inspire young people not only to discover and nurture the trailblazer within themselves but also to trust their imagination, even when it shows them a path that others say cannot exist, yet at the same time hold it to strict standards of proof. We hope they will form supportive relationships with others who share their vision, yet will also be willing to learn from those they compete with or even dislike. Above all, we hope they will feel the curiosity about the natural world and the determination to unravel its secrets that all trailblazers share.

Acknowledgments

I would like to thank Frank K. Darmstadt for his help and suggestions, Suzie Tibor for her hard work in rounding up the photographs, Bobbi McCutcheon for the outstanding line art, my cats for keeping me company (helpfully or otherwise), and, as always, my husband, Harry Henderson, for—well—everything.

Introduction

When Alfred Blalock, Helen Taussig, and Vivien Thomas revolutionized surgical treatment of the heart and nearby blood vessels in 1944, a more improbable partnership than the one that linked these three—a white male surgeon, a white female physician, and an African-American male laboratory technician—would have been hard to imagine. People of such different professions, genders, and races would have been unlikely in those days even to encounter one another, let alone work together.

Separately, each of these individuals was brilliant. Blalock discovered the cause and best treatment of the deadly medical condition called *shock,* which can occur after severe injury or loss of blood; Taussig essentially founded *pediatric cardiology,* the medical subspecialty dealing with children's heart ailments; and Thomas was an inventor and, according to those who knew him, close to being a surgical genius. It was the combination of their skills, however, that made medical history. Taussig's extensive knowledge of heart-related birth defects led her to think of a groundbreaking operation to help children who suffered from one of these defects, which kept most of their blood from reaching their lungs and therefore kept their bodies from receiving a sufficient supply of life-giving oxygen. Blalock then had the scientific insight to realize that he and Thomas had already performed this type of surgery for a different purpose on animals. Finally, Thomas used determination and skill to refine the operation to the point where it could be used on human beings. As William S. Stoney, writing in *Pioneers of Cardiac Surgery,* put it, "Taussig presented a unique original observation to the one person [actually two people] in the country who had the experimental background and surgical experience to see immediately that [the surgical treatment she proposed] could be done." The result was the *blue baby operation,* which rerouted blood vessels near the heart to allow more blood to reach the lungs. (The name came from the fact that the shortage of oxygen in the untreated children made their skin appear blue.) This operation not only saved thousands of children's lives but also made surgeons all over the world realize for the first time that operating on the heart, or at least the great blood vessels next to it, was possible.

SOCIAL OBSTACLES

The partnership of Blalock, Taussig, and Thomas was both nurtured and hindered by the institution in which it took place: the medical school and hospital of Johns Hopkins University in Baltimore, Maryland. Hopkins had the reputation of training outstanding surgeons such as Alfred Blalock from its beginning. Additionally, the wealthy Baltimore women who provided most of the school's funding in the early 1890s did so on the condition that it admit women "on the same terms as men," and so Hopkins became one of the few, if not the only, major medical school at the time that offered M.D. degrees to women. Hopkins certainly did not promote women on the same terms as men, however; it did not make Taussig a full professor until near the end of her illustrious career, and it had allowed only one other woman (Florence R. Sabin [1871–1953], promoted in 1917) to reach that rank before her.

As for African Americans, Hopkins did not go as far as Vanderbilt University in Nashville (where Blalock and Thomas worked during the early part of their careers), which classified all African-American employees as janitors. However, most of the Hopkins clinics and other facilities were segregated, and it was notorious for paying low wages to African-American workers. African Americans in professional positions were so rare that Vivien Thomas left a wave of open mouths and shocked expressions behind him when he walked down a public corridor in his white laboratory coat. As a black man without a college degree, let alone a medical education, Thomas had to fight throughout his career for sufficient pay to support himself and his family. When pushed hard enough, Blalock supported him in this effort—but, it seems, more because he was afraid of losing Thomas's surgical and research skills than out of any sense of racial injustice.

For most of Thomas's life, public recognition of his scientific efforts seemed beyond imagination. He ran the Hopkins surgical research laboratory for decades, yet other men held the official title of laboratory director. He taught surgical techniques to a generation of medical students, yet he was not a member of the Hopkins faculty. Only a few of the many researchers who received assistance from Thomas gave him credit in scientific papers, and Blalock was not one of them. Although Thomas received a few honors and rewards from Hopkins in his last years, his role in creating the blue baby operation was little known outside the institution until after his death. Even men who admired him showed an unconscious prejudice; numerous memoirs in Stoney's book, which was published in 2008, refer to Blalock as "Dr. Blalock" or "the Professor" but call Thomas only "Vivien." None of the writers of these autobiographical sketches seems to have noticed this difference.

INTERTWINING LIVES

In recounting the lives and careers of these three medical pioneers, which were sometimes separate and sometimes intertwined, this volume in the Trailblazers of Science and Technology set takes a chronological approach. Chapter 1 describes the early lives and education of Blalock, Taussig, and Thomas up to the year 1930, when Blalock and Taussig were about 30 years old and Thomas was 20. Chapter 2 covers the meeting of Blalock and Thomas and their research on shock at Vanderbilt University, as well as Helen Taussig's first studies of heart-related birth defects in children.

The focus changes to Johns Hopkins in chapter 3, which tells how Blalock became the Hopkins hospital's chief of surgery in 1941 and brought Thomas with him to Baltimore. Taussig, already working in Hopkins's pediatric heart clinic, began to think of a possible surgical treatment for certain birth defects at this time. As recounted in chapter 4, she presented her ideas to Blalock and Thomas, and they developed the blue baby operation from them. With Thomas standing behind him and giving advice, Blalock performed the surgery on its first human patient—a frail infant named Eileen Saxon—on November 29, 1944. The operation made worldwide headlines, and new patients and their families were soon "coming out of the walls."

Chapter 5, which carries the story to the end of the 1940s, describes the fame that the blue baby operation brought to Blalock and, to a lesser extent, Taussig; Blalock's trip to Europe to lecture on and demonstrate the surgery, for instance, became what an admirer called a "royal progress." The chapter also outlines the stress that developed between Blalock and Taussig as they struggled to provide the best possible care for their tiny patients. Thomas, meanwhile, continued to work quietly in his laboratory, demonstrating such skill that Blalock referred to one of his surgical repairs as looking like "something the Lord made."

In the 1950s, the subject of chapter 6, other surgeons—including some whom Blalock and Thomas had trained—carried heart surgery to the next stage by developing ways to stop the heart during operations without endangering patients. Blalock supported these advances but took no part in them; as chapter 7 explains, he died of cancer in 1964. Thomas and Taussig, however, continued their work at Hopkins. Taussig made another important contribution to medicine in 1962, when she helped to spread the word about the dangers that a supposedly harmless medication called thalidomide presented to pregnant women and their unborn children. Thomas finally received some of the recognition he deserved in the 1970s, including promotions and an honorary degree. He died in 1985 and Taussig in 1986.

The story of these three unlikely partners highlights social injustices of the mid-20th century that, to some extent, still exist. However, it also shows how individuals could work around these hindrances and combine their talents to create a medical advance that none of them would have been likely to create alone. Their work not only restored once hopelessly ill children to health, but also opened a new era in surgery.

Three Beginnings

As the oldest son in his family, 12-year-old Alfred Blalock had a special job to do when the family moved from Culloden, Georgia (where he had been born on April 5, 1899), to the larger town of Jonesboro: He had to leave a day ahead of the others so he could ride with their cow, Daisy, on the freight train to her new home. Alfred's father, George Z. Blalock, had run both a general store and the bank in the tiny hamlet of Culloden, as well as owning a large cotton farm. Blalock's health was poor, however, so in 1911 he decided to sell his land and businesses and move closer to the good medical care available in Atlanta. With him, in addition to the cow, came his wife, the former Martha Davis; Alfred, usually called Al; and the Blalocks' other two children, Edgar (born in 1901) and Elizabeth (born in 1905). The couple would later have two additional children, Mary (born in 1911) and Georgia (born in 1917).

A STRICT UPBRINGING

George Blalock did not work again after the family moved to Jonesboro, but his children told Alfred Blalock's friend and biographer, William P. Longmire, Jr. (1913–2003), that their father was well respected in both their family and the community. Georgia Blalock remembered her father as "autocratic, intelligent, well-informed, and well-read (classics), ambitious for his children, honest (almost to a fault), hard to please, demanding, and spoiled (by my mother)." (Longmire reprinted her words in his biography of Blalock, *Alfred Blalock: His Life and Times*.) Martha Blalock, 13 years younger than her husband, seldom dared to question his orders. However, her calmness and gentleness helped to counteract George Blalock's harshness.

Al Blalock learned self-control from having to follow his father's strict rules. He also learned to value education and academic success. Mark M. Ravitch (1910–89), another friend who learned surgery from Blalock at Johns Hopkins University, wrote in a biographical sketch at the beginning of *The Papers of Alfred Blalock* that young Al refused to go to bed until his homework was as perfect as he could make it. In spite of having to spend time on chores such as taking care of the cow, he did well in school. He was also popular with other students, especially girls, and played on both the tennis and the baseball teams in high school.

Blalock enrolled in Georgia Military Academy in Milledgeville, a preparatory school for the University of Georgia, at age 14. After a year there and some additional summer school classes, he moved on to the university, which he was able to enter as a sophomore in 1915. There he continued his sports career, winning a letter in tennis in his senior year and playing basketball as well. He was also on the university's debate team and yearbook staff. In spite of all these extracurricular activities, he managed to earn better-than-average grades. His favorite class, he wrote later, was zoology (the study of animals).

ROCKY START

Alfred Blalock told William Longmire that he had always expected to become a medical doctor: "My interest in medicine arose at such a young age that I cannot trace its development," he claimed in 1944. Blalock's brother and sisters, however, believed that their father gave Al the idea that he should be a physician. Certainly George Blalock told his son where he should take his medical training—Johns Hopkins University, in Baltimore, Maryland. The senior Blalock had had an operation there and was impressed by the university hospital's standard of patient care.

Blalock graduated from the University of Georgia in 1918, shortly after his 19th birthday, and entered the Johns Hopkins medical school that fall. In an autobiographical note quoted by Longmire, Blalock wrote that he "did not study as much as [he] should have" during most of his time at the school, choosing instead to spend much of his time socializing. He also worked at the student bookstore to earn money for his school expenses and continued to play sports, which now included golf as well as tennis. His sports activities

Alfred Blalock's father expected him to take his medical training at the medical school and hospital of Johns Hopkins University in Baltimore, Maryland. (A modern view of the hospital is shown here.) In time, Helen Taussig and Vivien Thomas would join Blalock in making medical history at Hopkins. *(Maxwell Boam, Johns Hopkins Medicine Marketing and Communication)*

introduced him to a fellow student named Tinsley Harrison (1900–78), who became his roommate and close friend. Blalock earned his M.D. degree in 1922.

Blalock graduated from Johns Hopkins in 1922 and, just as modern physicians still do, continued his training by working as a hospital *intern*. Inspired by the example of William Stewart Halsted (1852–1922), one of the "big four" physicians who had made the Johns Hopkins medical school famous, Blalock had decided to specialize in surgery, and he badly wanted to obtain an internship in general surgery at Johns Hopkins Hospital. Only the highest academic achievers in each medical school class were chosen for these internships, however, and Blalock's grades were not good enough to qualify. Instead, he was offered an internship divided among urology (the medical specialty that studies and treats the urinary tract), gynecology (the specialty that studies and treats medical conditions affecting women), and general surgery.

Blalock's failure to win the surgical internship—a shocking setback to someone used to doing reasonably well in school without making much effort—"stimulated [him] to get to work," he later told Longmire. Blalock had heard that Halsted, the hospital's chief of surgery, was interested in the gallbladder and its related body parts through which that organ produced bile, a substance that helps the digestive system break down fat. He therefore began to do research on the bile system, reviewing all the recent hospital cases that had involved it, in the hope that this activity would impress Halsted enough to give him the position of assistant *resident* (the next step up the training ladder) in general surgery the following year.

Blalock's investigation produced his first two scientific papers, a short one published in the *Journal of the American Medical Association* in 1924 and a longer one, "A Statistical Study of Eight Hundred and Eighty-Eight Cases of Biliary Tract Disease," which appeared in the *Johns Hopkins Hospital Bulletin* later in the same year. William Longmire wrote that these papers broke no new scientific ground, but they showed that Blalock was willing to work hard for what he wanted. He carried out that work in spite of being stricken with kidney disease serious enough to lead to the loss of one kidney on February 16, 1923.

THE LABORATORY BECKONS

In essence, Blalock's efforts succeeded. Halsted died before reading his papers, but the new acting chief of surgery, J. M. T. Finney, liked them well enough to offer Blalock the assistant residency in general surgery that he sought. Blalock's promotion troubles were not over, however. Because of his involvement in a dispute between some of the residents and their professors, his assistant residency in surgery was not renewed the following year, even though he did not really deserve this punishment. One of Blalock's professors, Samuel Crowe, rescued him by offering him an assistant residency in otolaryngology, the study of diseases of the ear and throat, which was Crowe's specialty.

During this second assistant residency, Blalock found his interests turning toward laboratory research for the first time. He was inspired partly by Crowe and partly by his friend and old roommate, Tinsley Harrison, who had recently returned to Hopkins as an assistant resident in medicine. Harrison had developed an enthusiasm for research during his internship years at Peter Bent Brigham Hospital in Boston, and he now passed that enthusiasm on to Blalock. Blalock published two papers with Crowe and two others with Harrison, all but one involving experiments on dogs carried out in 1924 and early 1925. Longmire writes that these papers were Blalock's first pieces of original laboratory work. True to form, the young surgeon added this new interest to his life without giving up any of his old ones. "Al had the willingness to work a hundred hours a week. He . . . would stay in the lab until midnight and then go out on a date," Harrison said in a 1973 interview.

Surgery was still Blalock's first love, however. He decided that he must have a residency in general surgery, even if he had to leave Hopkins to obtain it. Crowe persuaded renowned brain surgeon Harvey Cushing (1869–1939), then professor of surgery at Harvard University and chief of surgery at Peter Bent Brigham Hospital, to seek a position for Blalock there. Blalock agreed to go, but he felt ashamed at having to take another job that had been granted only as a favor.

A CHANGE OF DIRECTION

Just after Alfred Blalock arrived in Boston in June 1925—"before I even had time to unpack my trunk," he wrote later—he received a phone call from Tinsley Harrison that changed his plans completely. Harrison was about to become the chief resident in medicine at the new hospital attached to the recently reorganized Vanderbilt University medical school in Nashville, Tennessee, and he said that if Blalock joined him, Blalock could be the hospital's chief resident in surgery. Vanderbilt had nothing like the prestige of Johns Hopkins or Harvard, but the chance to win such an advanced position

Vanderbilt University, in Nashville, Tennessee, seemed like a "school in the backwoods" to Alfred Blalock when he went there in 1925 to become the university hospital's chief resident in surgery. In fact, however, the newly reorganized medical school and hospital would become famous for research achievements—including Blalock's own on shock. This photo shows the entrance to the Vanderbilt School of Medicine as Blalock would have seen it when he arrived. *(Historical Collection, Eskind Biomedical Library, Vanderbilt University Medical Center)*

seemed too good to miss. "I thought I was finished, going down to nowhere, to that school in the backwoods," Blalock said later. Still, "the future prospects [at Vanderbilt] looked brighter and more definite for me than they did if I remained in Boston." Blalock and his still-packed trunk therefore headed for Nashville.

Blalock's new job was supposed to begin on July 1, 1925. He found that the hospital was not quite ready for him, but the medical school's laboratory was. He and Tinsley Harrison therefore settled down to their favorite shared activity, research. Both were interested in the heart, so they decided to find out how that organ's output changed under various conditions. To do this, they employed the laboratory's new manometer, which measured the amount of oxygen and carbon dioxide in the blood. They compared the levels of these gases in the *arteries* with the levels in the *veins*. A second device, called a spirometer, measured the amount of oxygen that an animal consumed in a particular period of time. Once they knew these three measurements, Blalock and Harrison could use a mathematical formula to calculate the amount of blood that the heart pumped out in a unit of time. The two published a number of papers on *cardiac* output in 1927, based on work they did in 1925 and 1926.

RESEARCH ON SHOCK BEGINS

Although Alfred Blalock and Tinsley Harrison remained close friends, they soon found that their research interests were growing apart. Harrison wanted to study the heart itself, whereas Blalock preferred to investigate medical conditions related to surgery. In late 1926, therefore, they decided not to work together any longer.

Blalock chose to focus his studies on shock. This medical condition strikes people who have lost a large amount of blood, suffered severe injury or a surgical operation, or are gravely ill, for instance from a massive infection. When people go into shock, their skin becomes pale, cold, and clammy, their hearts beat rapidly but weakly, and they may pant or gasp for breath. They become confused and sometimes lose consciousness. Their blood pressure usually drops to undetectable levels. The condition can be fatal if left untreated.

During World War I, shock killed many soldiers who might otherwise have survived. It also caused high numbers of deaths among surgery patients. William Longmire wrote that, after anesthesia and ways to prevent infection were discovered in the 19th century, shock became "the greatest remaining impediment in the advance of surgery and the care of the injured."

Blalock first studied shock caused by loss of blood. After giving dogs morphine so that they would not feel pain, he drained blood from their bodies and then observed what happened to their circulation as they went into shock. Using the same techniques as in his earlier research with Harrison, he measured the dogs' oxygen consumption and the oxygen content of their blood and calculated their heart output at different times after shock was produced. He also tested the treatments for shock commonly used at the time. He concluded that the most important effects of shock were a sharp drop in the amount of blood the heart pumped and a constriction, or

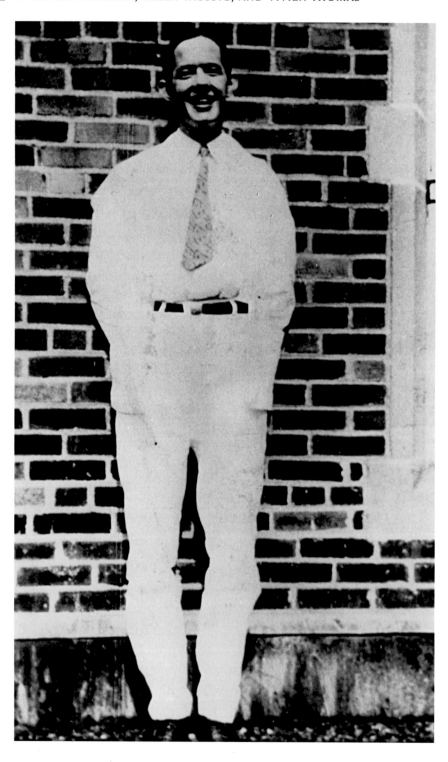

shrinking, of the arteries that carried blood. In essence, the circulation collapsed, leaving the body without the oxygen that it needed for life.

Blalock found that blood transfusion was by far the most effective treatment for shock caused by bleeding. If blood was not available, salt solution could be put into the blood vessels to restore the liquid that the circulation needed in order to function. Most drugs used to treat shock, by contrast, were useless or even harmful.

FORCED VACATION

Alfred Blalock needed every bit of his capacity for hard work to keep up with what had become a very demanding schedule. Once the Vanderbilt hospital opened in late 1925, he had to teach medical students and operate on patients there in addition to conducting his research. The hospital's chief of surgery, Barney Brooks (1884–1952), made Blalock an instructor in surgery (a junior faculty position), put him in charge of thoracic (chest) surgery in the hospital, and assigned him to run the experimental laboratory as well. As if all this were not enough, Blalock still played as hard as he worked. He later told Longmire that at this time he routinely stayed in the laboratory until midnight, then went out and partied until three or four o'clock in the morning.

By early 1927, Blalock found that even his seemingly inexhaustible energy had limits. Lack of sleep weakened his body's defenses against germs, and he contracted *tuberculosis*. This illness, caused by a bacterium, was common at the time. It usually attacked the lungs, making its victims gasp for breath, cough up blood, and sometimes die.

Blalock became so ill that, much to his frustration, he had to lay his work at Vanderbilt aside. In those days before antibiotics, the only treatment for tuberculosis was spending time in a sanatorium, a combination resort and hospital that provided medical care and bed rest in clean country air. Blalock decided to go to the Trudeau Sanatorium, in Saranac, New York, which treated many physicians and medical students who developed the disease. Tinsley Harrison traveled with him so that Blalock would have someone to help him if he became sicker during the journey. Harrison also promised to write the paper describing the shock research that Blalock had just finished.

The paper appeared later in the year in *Archives of Surgery* as "Mechanism and Treatment of Experimental Shock: I. Shock Following Hemorrhage." No one had ever described the process of shock as clearly or accurately as Blalock did in this paper. According to James M. McGreevy, a University of Utah surgeon writing in *Current Surgery* in 2003, the paper "made [Blalock] famous."

At Trudeau, Blalock wanted to try an aggressive tuberculosis treatment called pneumothorax, in which a surgeon would make a small hole in his chest and inject air under pressure to collapse his tubercular lung. Relieved of its breathing duties, the lung could rest and heal. The tradition-minded sanatorium doctors refused to allow this, however. They believed that pure, cold mountain air and rest were the only treatments that worked, and they made sure that Blalock had plenty of both. During his first 10 months at the sanatorium, he had to sleep on a porch outside the infirmary, even during the winter.

Blalock felt that neither air nor rest was doing him much good. He and some of the other residents of the seven-person cottage to which he was transferred after the 10 months developed a fatalistic attitude, assuming that they were going to die young no matter what they did. One of them, Norman Bethune (1890–1939), even painted a mural on the cottage wall that showed tombstones with their predicted dates of death. The date on Blalock's tomb-stone was 1929.

Blalock left Trudeau in early 1928. According to William Longmire, he decided that if he was going to die anyway, he would enjoy life while he could. He cashed in his insurance policy and used the money to finance a trip to Europe. Typically for Blalock, however, this was no mere vacation; he spent most of it visiting the laboratories of famous medical researchers.

A severe bout of bleeding from his lungs while he was in Germany frightened Blalock into remembering that he was still a very sick man. He returned to Saranac in midsummer and again pressured the doctors to give him pneumothorax treatments, and this time they agreed. The treatments worked well enough to let him return to Vanderbilt in September 1928, now with the rank of assistant professor. He continued the treatments for another year or so, carrying out his university duties at the same time. In spite of Bethune's and his own gloomy predictions, his health slowly returned.

Blalock had another reason to be happy at this time. Around 1929, Tinsley Harrison introduced him to Mary Chambers O'Brien, a young woman (more than 10 years younger than Blalock) who worked in the hospital's admitting office. Mark Ravitch, who knew O'Brien later, described her as "a beautiful, sparkling and vivacious Nashville belle." Blalock and O'Brien were very attracted to each other. With this new relationship, his restored health, a faculty promotion, and his experiments on shock beginning once more, Alfred Blalock had much to look forward to as the 1930s approached.

A STRUGGLE WITH READING

If Alfred Blalock had visited Boston just a few years earlier, his path might have crossed Helen Taussig's sooner than it did, because she grew up near there. Her father, Frank William Taussig (1859–1940), was a well-known professor of economics at Harvard and cofounder of the university's graduate school of business administration. Helen Brooke Taussig was born to Taussig and his wife, Edith Guild Taussig, on May 24, 1898. She was the youngest of the couple's four children. At her birth, her brother, William, was nine years old, and her sisters, Mary and Catherine, were six and two respectively. The family had a summer home on Cape Cod as well as a large house in Cambridge, the town (across the Charles River from Boston) in which Harvard is located.

Helen's mother, Edith, was one of the first graduates of Radcliffe, the college for women attached to Harvard; Harvard itself did not admit women. Edith had studied biology and botany in college and taught her daughter a love of nature, the outdoors, and gardening. When Helen was about nine years old, however, Edith developed tuberculosis. Less fortunate than Alfred Blalock, she died of the disease in 1909, when Helen was just 11 years old. Deprived of her mother, Helen formed a doubly close bond with her father.

Helen was an intelligent child, but she often did poorly in school because she had trouble with reading. Some later writers, including Joyce Baldwin, author of *To Heal the Heart of a Child,* a biography of Taussig for young adults (which is the only book-length biography of Taussig), have concluded that she had *dyslexia,* a learning disability that makes reading extremely difficult. Only her father's patience and belief in her let young Helen survive her school years without losing her self-confidence. Fortunately, however, the problem became less severe as she grew older.

Following in her mother's footsteps, Helen Taussig entered Radcliffe in 1917. Like Alfred Blalock, she enjoyed tennis, at which she became the college champion, and other sports, including basketball. She also liked drama.

Taussig was not really happy at Radcliffe, however. For one thing, she said later, "At Radcliffe I was known as my father's daughter" rather than as an individual with strengths and weaknesses of her own. During the summer before her sophomore year, she went with her father to the University of California at Berkeley, where he was teaching a summer school course, and she decided that she liked that university better than Radcliffe. She transferred there at the end of her sophomore year and earned her bachelor's degree from Berkeley in 1921.

DISSECTING A HEART

Helen Taussig was not sure what she should do after graduation. She had some interest in medicine as a career, but her father recommended that she study public health instead because he thought it was "a good field for women." She therefore applied to Harvard's School of Public Health.

Public health might be a good field for women, but Taussig quickly found out that Harvard had no interest in training them to enter it. The school's dean informed her that she could take courses there, but she would never be allowed to earn a degree. "Who is going to be such a fool as to spend two years studying medicine and two years more in public health and not get a degree?" Taussig asked him angrily.

"No one, I hope," replied the dean.

"Dr. Rosen, I will not be the first to disappoint you," said Taussig, marching out of the room. "Then and there, I went back and told my father that I was going to study medicine," she recalled in an interview published in *Today's Health* in August 1968.

In spite of her sharp words to the dean, Taussig decided that taking a course or two at Harvard Medical School might be a good idea. The next year, therefore, she signed up for a class in histology, the study of the microscopic structure of the body and its tissues. She was the only woman in the class, and she had to sit apart from her classmates in the lecture hall and do laboratory work in a separate room so that she would not "contaminate" the male students.

Taussig's histology teacher was impressed with her work and recommended that she transfer to nearby Boston University. There she could take a class in *anatomy,* a course she was not allowed to enroll in at Harvard, and obtain a full year's credit for her work. When she did so, Alexander Begg, her anatomy professor, was also struck by her intelligence. One day he startled Taussig by thrusting a beef heart into her hand. "Here, it won't do you any harm to become interested in one of the larger organs of the body," Begg told her.

Alexander Begg, a professor at Boston University who taught an anatomy class that Helen Taussig attended, startled her one day by thrusting a beef heart like this one into her hand and saying, "Here, it won't do you any harm to become interested in one of the larger organs of the body." Taussig's dissection of that heart began her lifelong interest in cardiology. (*Ugorenkov Aleksandr, 2009, used under license from Shutterstock, Inc.*)

Following Begg's advice, Taussig began dissecting the heart. She found its structure so interesting that she was inspired to begin her first research project, a study of the way heart muscle contracts, or pulls itself together and shrinks. Other researchers had shown that strips of muscle from reptiles and other cold-blooded animals contracted and relaxed rhythmically in a nutrient solution, but no one had demonstrated the same behavior in muscle from the heart of a mammal.

Taussig became so involved in her experiments that she often stayed in the laboratory until midnight. (The ability to work long hours was another characteristic she shared with Alfred Blalock.) Trying various solutions and

THE FIRST WOMEN DOCTORS

Before the 20th century, women were barred by custom and frequently by law from working as physicians. Authorities sometimes threatened those who disobeyed with death. People were sure that even the most inept male doctor would be more competent than the most brilliant woman.

Elizabeth Blackwell (1821–1910), the first woman in modern times to earn an M.D. degree, was able to enter medical school only because the people who saw her application thought it was a joke. When the dean of the Geneva Medical College, a small college in upstate New York, read Blackwell's letter to the school's students in 1847, they assumed that it had been sent by a rival college as a prank. Going along with the gag, as they believed, they sent back a solemn "unanimous invitation" for Blackwell to attend—and were utterly amazed when she actually appeared. She stayed to receive her degree on January 23, 1849. She went on to found the New York Infirmary for Women and Children, the first hospital staffed entirely by women, and a medical college for women.

Women physicians were no longer so unheard of by the time Helen Taussig began to consider a medical career, but they were still rare. Most medical schools did not admit women, and even the most eminent women physicians were often badly treated. In 1919, for example, Harvard University hired Alice Hamilton (1869–1970), who essentially founded industrial medicine in the United States, to teach that subject in its School of Public Health, becoming the first woman on the university's faculty—but it forbade her to enter the faculty club or march in the yearly commencement procession. Hamilton was still on the school's faculty, in the lowly rank of assistant professor, when Dean Rosen so abruptly rejected Taussig's application to become a student there.

heart tissue from a variety of animals, she eventually showed that the muscle did indeed beat rhythmically. Her work was published as a paper, "Rhythmic Contractions in Isolated Strips of Mammalian Ventricles," in the *American Journal of Physiology* in 1925.

"ON THE SAME TERMS AS MEN"

Alexander Begg told Helen Taussig to apply to the one highly respected medical school that *would* give a woman a doctor's degree: Johns Hopkins. Mary Elizabeth Garrett, the Baltimore railroad heiress who provided most of the money to build the school, had made it a condition of her bequests in the early 1890s that, as she stated, "women shall enjoy all the advantages of the Medical School of the Johns Hopkins University on the same terms as men."

Railroad heiress Mary Garrett (on far left) and the other wealthy Baltimore women (Carey Thomas, Mamie Gwinn, Bessie King, and Julia Rogers, left to right in this photograph) who provided most of the funding to build the Johns Hopkins medical school and hospital made it a condition of their bequests that women "enjoy all the advantages" of the school "on the same terms as men." Thanks to them, Hopkins was one of the few, if not the only, major U.S. medical school in the 1920s that admitted women. *(Bryn Mawr College Library)*

Edwards Albert Park (1877–1969), shown here in a painting by Paul Trebilcock in 1937, took over the pediatric department at the Johns Hopkins medical school and hospital in 1927. He became Helen Taussig's mentor and friend and appointed her to head his newly established pediatric cardiology clinic in 1930. (*Alan Mason Chesney Medical Archives of the Johns Hopkins Medical Institutions; photograph by Aaron Levin*)

Johns Hopkins accepted Taussig's application in 1924, and she earned her M.D. in 1927.

In arranging her postdoctoral training, Taussig encountered a disappointment much like Blalock's. She, too, had hoped for an internship at Johns Hopkins Hospital, but only one such prize was earmarked for a woman, and it went to the single female classmate whose grades had outstripped hers. Like Blalock, however, she found a way to remain at Hopkins. She had continued her interest in the heart by working in the hospital's heart clinic during medical school, and her supervisor there obtained a fellowship in *cardiology* for her. A year later, she won a two-year internship in *pediatrics,* the medical specialty that treats children.

Bad news was followed by good. Shortly after Taussig learned that she had lost the coveted internship, a former Yale University medical professsor, Edwards Albert Park, was appointed to head the pediatric department at Hopkins. He soon became Taussig's mentor and friend. A strong believer in specialty clinics, which treated only a single type or related group of medical conditions, Park decided that children with heart problems needed to have such a clinic. He therefore established a pediatric cardiac clinic in the Harriet Lane Home for Invalid Children, part of the Hopkins hospital complex, and assigned Taussig to work there. When she completed her pediatric internship in 1930, he helped her obtain an appointment as an assistant in pediatrics at the hospital and, more important, chose her to head the clinic. At the start of the 1930s, therefore, Helen Taussig's future seemed bright.

HOPES DEFERRED

Unlike Alfred Blalock and Helen Taussig, but like most other African Americans of his time, Vivien Theodore Thomas had almost no academic background. He was born in Lake Providence, a small town in northeastern Louisiana, on August 29, 1910. It is not completely clear why he was given what is usually considered to be a woman's name, but he often joked that it happened because his parents, who already had had a girl followed by two boys, expected their fourth child to be a girl.

Lake Providence, near the Mississippi River, suffered floods nearly every spring. In 1912, therefore, a year after Alfred Blalock led the family cow to Jonesboro, Vivien Thomas's parents, William Maceo Thomas and Mary Eaton Thomas, abandoned Lake Providence and moved their family to Nashville. Northwest Nashville was a thriving area, home of many middle-class African Americans—doctors, lawyers, and others, working mainly in their own community. The city had several respected black colleges, including Fisk University and Meharry Medical College, one of the two accredited medical schools in the country that admitted African Americans.

William Thomas, a skilled carpenter, had no trouble finding work in Nashville. He soon earned enough money to buy a large lot and build a house on it. Vivien, meanwhile, studied at the public schools in his community and graduated from Pearl High School in 1929. He also learned carpentry from his father, and he was able to work construction jobs on his own by the time he was 16.

Some of these jobs taught Thomas life lessons as well as work skills, Thomas explained in his autobiography, *Pioneering Research in Surgical Shock and Cardiovascular Surgery* (later reissued with the less wordy title *Partners of the Heart*). During a summer job on a building project at Fisk University in 1929, the construction crew's foreman assigned him to replace part of a house's damaged flooring with new wood. After inspecting the work the next day, the foreman said, "Thomas, that won't do. I can tell you put it in"—in other words, he could see where the new wood met the old. Thomas spent hours redoing the work, making the joins between the old wood and the replacement invisible. "I never had to repeat or redo another assignment," Thomas wrote proudly.

The foreman said little when he saw Thomas's improved work, but he rewarded the young man in a more practical way by keeping him on when he let the rest of the crew go at the end of the summer. This extra work proved to be vital for Thomas. Inspired by a family physician he had known as a child, Thomas had decided that he wanted to become a doctor, and he wanted to begin premedical study at nearby Tennessee State College. At first, he expected that the offered job would help him cover his college expenses. In October, however, the nation's stock market crashed, beginning the Great Depression of the 1930s, and Thomas found that he needed the money simply to survive.

The new decade might have seemed promising to Alfred Blalock and Helen Taussig, but for Vivien Thomas its prospects were grim. Like many others, he lost his job in October when the market collapsed. It was obvious that he would have to put his college plans aside for the time being, but he promised himself that they would not stay on hold forever. As he wrote in his autobiography, he determined that "I was going to find a job and . . . I would not be choosey about the nature of that job. There had to be something besides carpentry that I could do."

Lifesaving Research

Alfred Blalock was coming to the conclusion that other physicians did not understand shock at all. Most thought the condition was caused by a poison that the injured tissues released into the blood, but the experiments that Blalock had conducted on dogs after he returned to Vanderbilt convinced him that this idea was wrong. Loss of fluid from the blood was the important thing, he decided, even when shock was produced by injuries that did not cause bleeding. Conditions that resulted in shock somehow made blood vessels porous, allowing the liquid in the blood to leak out and pool in the body's tissues. Deprived of this fluid, the blood could not circulate, causing death from lack of oxygen.

GROUNDBREAKING DISCOVERY

Other researchers had noticed that liquid was lost from the bloodstream during shock, but they could not determine where it went, and they did not believe that the loss was great enough to cause the shock. Blalock's experiments said otherwise. He used anesthesia to put his dogs into a deep sleep so they could not feel pain, then injured one side of their bodies in various ways. After about eight hours, he killed the dogs, cut their bodies into quarters, and weighed each piece.

Similar experiments had been performed before, but the scientists who carried them out had compared the weight only of injured and uninjured limbs. Blalock, however, noticed that swelling caused by injury to a leg extended beyond the leg into the dog's torso. He therefore chose to weigh part of the torso as well as the limb. The earlier researchers had found no difference in weight between injured and uninjured legs, but when Blalock weighed the whole quarters of the dogs' bodies, the injured quarter proved to be much heavier than the uninjured one on the other side. This showed that a substantial amount of fluid leaked into the tissues after injury—most likely enough to make the blood circulation fail. If the injury was too mild to produce major leakage of fluid, shock did not occur.

By 1930, the paper describing these revolutionary experiments was almost ready for publication. Blalock's hospital and administrative duties were becoming more and more demanding, however, leaving him much less time in the laboratory than he would have liked. To make that small amount of time stretch farther, he realized that he had to have help. The lab's two assistants, Sam Waters and Isaac Bodie, took care of the dogs and helped to set up experiments, but Blalock wanted something more. He needed a personal assistant skilled enough not only to set up experiments but, under Blalock's direction, perform some of them himself.

A JOB OPENS UP

What Vivien Thomas needed was a job. In February 1930, during the first winter of the Great Depression, few of those were to be had, particularly in construction. Determined to accept anything, Thomas asked a friend who worked at Vanderbilt if he knew of any openings there. The friend said he had heard that one of the medical school physicians, Alfred Blalock, was looking for a laboratory assistant—but, the friend warned, Blalock had a quick temper and sometimes could be difficult.

Thomas did not care, as long as the temper came with a paycheck attached. On February 10, his friend took him to Blalock's office for a meeting. Drinking a Coca-Cola and smoking a cigarette—two items that, Thomas soon learned, the surgeon was seldom without—Blalock questioned the younger man about his family, education, and plans for the future. Thomas told him about his hopes of going to medical school. Blalock, in turn, explained what he was looking for in an assistant.

The surgeon then gave the young African American a tour of the laboratory. Blalock had an experiment set up in one corner of the lab, and he carefully explained to Thomas (as Thomas recalled in his autobiography) "what was being done, how it was being done, and why it was being done." Thomas, who had never been in a laboratory before, found the activities so interesting that he stayed on after Blalock left, watching Waters and Bodie perform their work.

When Blalock returned a little while later, the two men agreed that Thomas would try the job. Thomas was unhappy about the rate of pay being offered—$12 a week, less than two-thirds of the $20 per week that he had been earning on the Fisk crew—but Blalock promised that he would raise the rate in a few months if Thomas did well.

The next day, Blalock showed Thomas how to weigh a dog to determine how much anesthetic it would need, give the drug to the animal, and prepare it and the equipment for surgery. He then told Thomas that next morning he was to come in and prepare a dog for surgery on his own.

After Blalock left the room, the thunderstruck Thomas asked Sam Waters if the doctor had really meant what he said. "Sure, he expects you to do it," Waters answered. "He won't show you but once."

Fortunately, Thomas was a quick learner. Once—plus a little assistance and moral support from the experienced Sam—proved to be all he needed.

MUTUAL RESPECT

Over the next several months, the same routine was repeated with many procedures. Blalock dropped in to check on Thomas's progress, asked him questions, and reminded him to "keep your eyes open and write things down." Within a few weeks, he had Thomas beginning surgeries on his own.

Thomas almost always performed his tasks flawlessly. Once, however, he made a mistake and suddenly found himself on the receiving end of the sharp temper that his friend had warned him about. "The profanity [Blalock] used would have made the proverbial sailor proud of him," Thomas wrote in his autobiography.

Thomas simply stood there and let Blalock shout. Then, after the doctor had finally stalked out of the room, Thomas went to the laboratory's locker room, changed into his street clothes, and returned to Blalock's office.

Blalock looked up and greeted him "as though nothing had happened." Thomas quickly made it clear that he did not feel the same way. "I said that I had not been brought up to take or use the kind of language he had used across the hall." If Blalock was going to behave like that, Thomas went on, he would take his pay and seek work elsewhere.

Perhaps startled to be answered back in this way—especially by an African American—Blalock apologized and promised to be more careful of his language in the future. He urged Thomas to stay on, and, somewhat reluctantly, Thomas agreed.

"Just watch, he'll do the same thing again," Sam Waters told Thomas cynically—but for once, Waters was wrong. Thomas wrote the following many years later:

> Dr. Blalock kept his word for the next thirty-four years. . . . We had occasional disagreements and sometimes almost heated discussions, but . . . in retrospect, I think this incident set the stage for what I consider our mutual respect throughout the years.

In time, that respect ripened into friendship. Alcohol was illegal at the time, thanks to the Eighteenth Amendment to the U.S. Constitution, passed in 1919 (it was repealed in 1933 by the Twenty-first Amendment), but Blalock kept a 10-gallon (37.9-L) keg of whiskey hidden in the laboratory's storeroom and often had a drink from it, mixed with Coca-Cola, at the end of the day. Now and then he shared his illicit cocktail with Thomas—something that the two could never have done in public because of their different races.

The friendship was not without its strains, however, and most of them concerned Thomas's paycheck. That issue first came up in May 1930, after Thomas heard about a construction job opening at Fisk University. Thomas still viewed his laboratory work as merely a way to get by until better-paying jobs like this appeared, so he told Blalock that he was quitting.

By that time, Blalock apparently had realized what a find the young African American was. He did his best to persuade Thomas to stay, listing all the advantages he saw laboratory work as having over construction. That was all very well, Thomas said, but he had to earn "a living wage." Blalock asked Thomas how much he would make at Fisk, and when Thomas told him, he answered in the whiny tone for which he would later become famous, "We can't pay that kind of money. How much will you stay here for?" He promised to speak to the chief of surgery, Barney Brooks, about obtaining a raise. Blalock, Brooks, and Thomas finally compromised on $17.50 a week, a little over halfway between what Thomas had been making and what he could have earned at Fisk.

Meanwhile, Thomas's education continued. Joseph Beard, a young physician who joined the laboratory in July 1930, taught Thomas chemistry, anatomy, and physiology, the study of the body's functions. Beard also explained why it was so important in scientific experiments to understand what one was doing and why it was being done and to make precise and repeated measurements. Inspired by Beard and Blalock's enthusiasm, Thomas began to see his laboratory work as more than just a temporary job.

A PIVOTAL YEAR

In many ways, 1930 was a key year for Alfred Blalock. In addition to meeting Vivien Thomas, he advanced to the position of associate professor at Vanderbilt. He also married Mary O'Brien on October 25 in a ceremony that all accounts agree was a high point of that year's social season in Nashville. The couple eventually had three children: William Rice, born in 1931; Mary Elizabeth (Betty), born in 1933; and Alfred Dandy, born in 1943.

Most important for his career, Blalock's key paper on the causes of shock, "Experimental Shock: The Cause of the Low Blood Pressure Produced by Muscle Injury," was published in *Archives of Surgery* in June 1930. This paper and others that soon followed made medical history. Blalock—barely past his 30th birthday—completely rewrote physicians' understanding of shock. A few other researchers were obtaining similar results, but none presented the fluid-loss theory with as much supporting evidence as Blalock.

The year 1930 was important to Vivien Thomas too, but in a much less pleasant way. For most of the year, he clung to the hope that he would soon be able to return to college and go on to medical school, even though his job with Blalock paid too little to let him add anything to his savings. In November, however, the bank that held his savings failed, taking all his money with it. "My first feeling was anger—real anger, followed by a mixture of disbelief, resentment, disgust, and hate. Lingering in the background was a loss of trust in everything and everybody," he wrote.

Thomas's practical side quickly made him realize that he still had one precious thing: paying work. "Men were walking the streets looking for jobs that did not exist," he reminded himself. "For the time being, I felt somewhat secure in that, at least, I had a job." He occasionally discussed his hopes with Blalock, but Blalock "never encouraged me to attempt to continue my education," Thomas wrote. The surgeon, it seemed, was more interested in keeping a valuable laboratory technician than in helping that technician achieve his own dreams. By 1932, Thomas had set the thought of medical school aside, seemingly for good.

NEW EXPERIMENTS ON SHOCK

Vivien Thomas helped Alfred Blalock with surgical procedures during his first years in the laboratory. Then, beginning around 1933, Blalock taught him how to do "real surgery." Thomas learned the procedure for "scrubbing up" and putting on a sterile cap, gown, and mask—just as important for operating on dogs as on humans, since a dog that became ill or died from an infection caught during surgery was useless as part of an experiment. He learned how to make the incisions that began the operations and watched Blalock's movements as the experienced surgeon took over. He learned to sew, or *suture*, the dog's organs, muscles, and skin back together after the surgery was complete.

Blalock was happy to both encourage and take advantage of Thomas's growing abilities as his assistant. He came into the laboratory later and later, perhaps guessing what might—and finally did—happen. One day in 1935, Thomas made an incision on an unconscious dog before Blalock's arrival, as he was used to doing, then covered the wound and waited for the surgeon. And waited . . . and waited. "After forty-five minutes, when he still had not come, I went ahead with the procedure and slowly and painstakingly struggled on through alone," Thomas wrote in his autobiography. Blalock arrived only as Thomas was preparing to sew up the dog at the end of the operation. Increasingly often after that, Blalock—just as he had done earlier with the laboratory procedures—showed Thomas how to do an operation only once, then expected Thomas to do it on his own or with the help of a medical student.

Some critics had said that Blalock's first proof of his shock theory was too crude. Blalock therefore—with Vivien Thomas's increasingly expert help—made more detailed studies in the early 1930s, showing exactly which chemicals were lost in the fluid that oozed out of the blood vessels and which ones remained in the circulation. Thomas made many of the chemical measurements.

Blalock's chemistry experiments showed why shock is so disastrous to the body. The key substances that leak out of the vessels with the fluid during shock, he explained in a lecture in Chicago in 1933, are *proteins,* a large class of biochemicals that do most of the work of the body. Certain proteins attract fluid and keep it in place. When these proteins drain into the tissues through the leaky blood vessels, fluid from the blood follows them, leaving the circulation depleted.

Blalock also made further studies of different treatments for shock. He examined various types of fluid and ways of giving them, as well as treatment by drugs, heat, and cold. Reinforcing his earlier conclusion about shock caused by bleeding, his new experiments indicated that the best treatment for any type of shock is replacing the fluid lost from the bloodstream, either by blood transfusions or by giving just the liquid part of the blood, called *plasma.*

Although some experts continued to question his conclusions for several years, Alfred Blalock's research ultimately changed the way surgeons and physicians treated shock as well as their understanding of its causes. Fluid replacement saved many lives in the operating room, and it would go on to save many more during World War II. Even near the end of his career, when he had achieved so much, Blalock often said that his work on shock was his most important contribution to medicine. Some others have agreed. In 1965, in an obituary article on Blalock, H. William Scott of the Nashville Surgical Society wrote, "The principles [Blalock] established in the management of shock have probably saved more lives than any other scientific contribution made by a surgeon."

ONLY A JANITOR

Vivien Thomas's salary became an issue again around 1935. By this time, Thomas was supporting more than just himself. On December 22, 1933, he had married Clara Beatrice Flanders, an attractive young woman he had met the previous summer when visiting his sister in Macon, Georgia, and they now had a baby daughter, Olga Fay. (They would have a second daughter, Theodosia Patricia, in 1938.)

Thomas and James Lewis, Tinsley Harrison's laboratory technician, who was also an African American, wondered one day whether they received the same pay as white technicians who did the same kinds of work. Lewis persuaded a talkative secretary to tell him how much one of the white technicians earned, and it indeed proved to be far more than he and Thomas were paid. Armed with this information, Thomas spoke to the business manager, who said that Thomas earned less because he had a lower job classification. Vanderbilt University, he explained, classified all African American as janitors, no matter what kind of work they actually performed.

Understandably angry, Thomas told Blalock what he had learned. He understood that Blalock might not be able to make the school change his classification, but perhaps, he said, the doctor could do something about his

(continued on page 28)

BLOOD GOES TO WAR

In the early 1930s, when Alfred Blalock did most of his groundbreaking research on shock, transfusions of blood or plasma—the treatments for shock that he recommended—were possible, but they were not yet widely available. Blalock's discoveries about shock helped bring them into common use.

Blood transfusions had become potentially safe after the Austrian physician Karl Landsteiner (1868–1943) discovered *blood types* (or blood groups) in 1901. Landsteiner found that red blood cells had substances called antigens on their surfaces. Depending on the kinds of antigens they possessed, humans could be divided into four groups: A, B, AB, or O. If people were given blood containing an antigen that their own blood did not carry, their *immune system* (the body's defense system) attacked the donor blood, causing severe illness or even death. This reaction could be predicted by mixing a few drops of donor and recipient blood on a microscope slide before the transfusion. If cells in the mixed blood formed clumps, the transfusion was not safe; if clumping did not occur, the transfusion could proceed.

Transfusions still were not common, however, because no one knew how to store blood. It quickly formed clots, gooey masses that made it

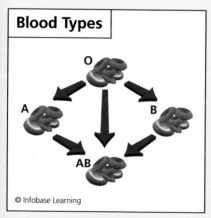

Blood Types

O

A   B

AB

© Infobase Learning

Karl Landsteiner and his coworkers discovered around 1900 that each person belongs to one of four main blood types or groups: A, B, AB, or O. Anyone can safely give blood to or receive blood from anyone else belonging to the same group. People belonging to group O can give blood to anyone but can receive blood only from other type O people. People of types A and B can give blood to people of type AB but not to each other. People of type AB can receive blood from anyone but can give it only to other type AB people.

useless for transfusion. (This was a different reaction from the clumping seen when different blood types were mixed.) Researchers discovered in 1914 that adding a chemical called sodium citrate to blood could preserve it for up to 10 days, but that was not very long. Only around the time of Blalock's shock experiments did scientists learn that refrigeration could extend this preservation time to a month or more. Bernard Fantus (1874–1940), a Chicago physician, used this technique in 1937 to create what he called a blood bank.

Blood banks also stored plasma, the liquid part of the blood. Plasma did not contain antigens, so it did not have to be tested for type. It could be preserved in liquid form for much longer than whole blood. In 1935, furthermore, researchers found that plasma could be freeze-dried and

(continued)

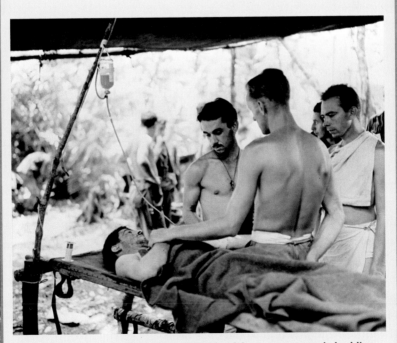

Infusions of plasma, the liquid part of the blood, kept many wounded soldiers from dying of shock during World War II. Plasma could be freeze-dried, stored as a powder, and reconstituted with sterile water when needed. This photograph shows U.S. soldiers administering plasma to a wounded soldier at a field hospital in New Guinea. *(Library of Congress)*

(continued)

stored as a powder. "Plasma kits" consisting of a small bottle of plasma flakes, a pint of sterile water, tubing, and a hypodermic needle traveled with soldiers and battlefield medical crews in World War II. If a soldier was wounded, the powder could be quickly mixed with the water and injected.

Soldiers nearly dead from shock would receive plasma transfusions and a few minutes later according to one wartime report, "would be sitting up and talking, with all the life and color back in their faces." With their blood volume restored, they could survive long enough to reach more extensive medical help. Partly because of the wider availability of blood and plasma, the death rate among wounded soldiers in World War II was less than half that in World War I.

(continued from page 25)

salary. It was not enough to let him support a new family, and if he was doing a technician's work, he should receive a technician's pay.

Blalock reacted as he had done before, and would do again, when Thomas brought up such topics. He made a vague promise to see what he could do, then never mentioned the matter again. This time, however, a change occurred. Thomas and Lewis never knew whether their classification had been revised—they felt it was wiser not to ask—but after a few months, they found that their pay had quietly increased. It still was not equal to that of white Vanderbilt technicians, but it was certainly more than a mere janitor would receive. Thomas felt that this one-on-one approach had succeeded where a broader-based, more organized protest would have failed. "Had there been an organized complaint by the Negroes performing technical duties," he wrote in his autobiography, "there was a good chance that all kinds of excuses would have been offered to avoid giving us technicians' pay and that leaders of the movement or action would have been summarily fired."

A SINGLE MIND

By this time, Blalock and Thomas worked together so well that the medical students who spent time in their laboratory saw them as almost "a single mind." One of those students, Rollin Daniel, wrote in 1966:

Most of the preparations [the operations in the experiments] were carried out by Vivien. Dr. Blalock would think the thing through. He and Vivien would operate together on a dog, or a few dogs, and then Vivien would take over, Dr. Blalock dropping by, making suggestions and corrections and Vivien performing the operative procedures and setting up the experiments with tremendous care and attention to detail.

Thomas's "manual skill at involved operative procedures [became] legendary," Mark Ravitch wrote in his biographical sketch of Alfred Blalock.

An incident in 1937 showed how much Blalock had come to value Thomas's laboratory and surgical skills. The Henry Ford Hospital in Detroit, Michigan, offered Blalock the position of chief of surgery. Blalock said he would accept the offer only if he was allowed to bring Thomas with him as his assistant. The hospital had a policy of not hiring African Americans, however, and it refused. Blalock, in turn, rejected the position at Ford, even though it would have been more prestigious than his job at Vanderbilt. In

During their years at Vanderbilt University, Vivien Thomas and Alfred Blalock learned to work so well together that students who spent time in their laboratory thought of them as "a single mind." Thomas is shown here in the laboratory at Vanderbilt in the 1930s. (*Historical Collection, Eskind Biomedical Library, Vanderbilt University Medical Center*)

that same year, perhaps in the hope of encouraging Blalock not to leave, Vanderbilt promoted him to the rank of full professor.

In the late 1930s, in addition to continuing their work on shock, Blalock and Thomas began investigating high blood pressure, sometimes called "the silent killer" because it produces few signs of illness but can lead to fatal heart attacks and strokes. In the course of these experiments, they taught themselves the delicate art of stitching blood vessels together, a skill that few surgeons knew.

In order to study an illness like high blood pressure, Blalock and Thomas first had to produce the condition in their dogs. In 1938, with the help of Sanford Levy, a young physician who had joined the laboratory in 1936, they tried to create high blood pressure in a dog's lungs by joining the *pulmonary artery,* which brings blood from the right side of the heart to the lungs, and the *subclavian artery,* the main artery that carries blood to the arms in humans and the front legs in dogs. They expected this rerouting to raise pressure in the lungs because blood going to the body as a whole, including the blood in the subclavian artery, is under much higher pressure than that going through the pulmonary artery. Although the surgery was successful, it did not produce the change in blood pressure that they were looking for, so they set the procedure aside. They had no idea how useful it would prove to be in just a few years.

LISTENING HANDS

Meanwhile, at Johns Hopkins, Helen Taussig's career was also turning in a new direction. But first, as Blalock had done near the start of his days at Vanderbilt, Taussig had to face a severe health challenge. Around 1930, just after she took over the new pediatric cardiology clinic at the Harriet Lane Home, she suddenly lost most of her hearing. No one was ever sure why, but a bout of whooping cough, then a contagious disease common in children, may have been the cause.

Taussig's deafness deprived her of some of the things she enjoyed, such as music. It also greatly hampered her work in the clinic. Like most physicians, she was used to diagnosing heart problems chiefly by listening through a stethoscope, which amplified the sound of the heartbeat. Now that tool was no longer available to her. Stethoscopes with built-in sound boosters helped, but they were not enough.

One important substitute was the *fluoroscope,* a machine that used X-rays passing through the body to create a glowing image of the heart,

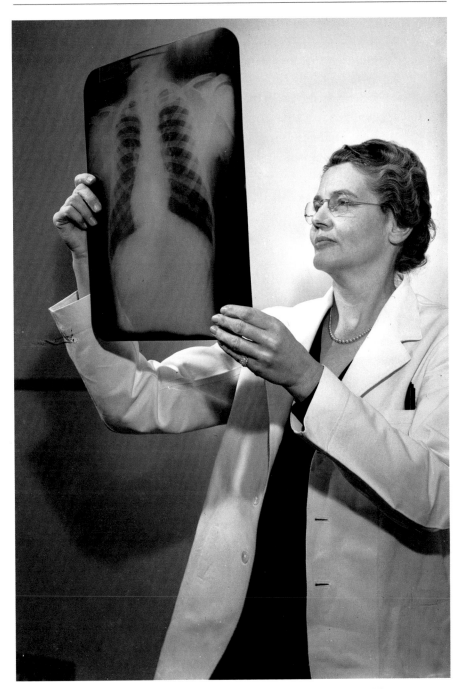

After Helen Taussig lost her hearing around 1930, she relied mostly on X-ray and fluoroscope images and on her sensitive hands to identify heart problems in children. Taussig is shown here examining a child's chest X-ray in 1946. *(B771A; the Maryland Historical Society)*

lungs, and major blood vessels on a screen. When Taussig wanted to examine a child with this device, she placed the child between the fluoroscope and the screen. By having her young patient take different positions, she could observe the size and shape of its heart and attached blood vessels from different angles. Sometimes she asked the child to swallow a substance called barium (blended into chocolate pudding to disguise its chalky taste), in order to make the outlines in the fluoroscope pictures clearer.

More uniquely, Taussig taught herself to "listen" with her hands. She became extremely sensitive to the vibrations that her little patients' beating hearts produced in their chests. Her gentle touch calmed the often-frightened children who came to her, but few of them realized that it also helped her learn exactly what was wrong with them.

BORN WITH BAD HEARTS

Most of the children that Helen Taussig saw in her clinic during the early 1930s had hearts injured by *rheumatic fever.* This illness sometimes followed an attack of *strep throat,* an infection caused by a common type of bacteria called streptococcus. The bacteria sometimes left the throat after several weeks and attacked the joints and heart valves. As with tuberculosis and so many other infectious diseases, there was no treatment for rheumatic fever in the days before antibiotics except rest.

Busy as he knew she was with the rheumatic fever children, Edwards Park, Taussig's supervisor and mentor, wanted to broaden her perspective. "Now, Taussig, you're going to learn *congenital* malformations of the heart," he said to her one day as they waited for an elevator. Taussig protested that she had neither time nor interest in learning about heart problems that arose from birth defects. "It doesn't make any difference how you feel," Park replied. "You're going to learn about them, and when you do, it will be a great day."

Taussig certainly had seen some of these children at the Harriet Lane clinic. They were easy to recognize because their lips, noses, ears, and fingernails—indeed, sometimes their whole bodies—were blue. Taussig knew that this blue color, called *cyanosis,* occurred because the children's blood did not contain enough oxygen. *Hemoglobin,* the pigment in blood that carries oxygen, is bright red when it is fully loaded with that lifegiving gas, but when it is depleted of oxygen, it turns bluish. That is why blood in the veins, which has given up its oxygen to body cells, looks blue, while blood in the arteries, which has recently received oxygen, is red. In children with the most common kinds of inborn heart defects, all the blood was blue.

The Canadian physician Maude Abbott (1869–1940), shown here, was the world's greatest expert on birth defects affecting the heart in the late 1930s. Helen Taussig visited Abbott in Montreal in 1938 to learn more about these defects. (*National Library of Medicine*)

Taussig eventually took Park's advice and began to look more closely at children with these defects. She learned to recognize the images that different kinds of heart defects produced on the fluoroscope screen. More than anyone before her, she realized that particular birth defects made such similar pictures that fluoroscope or X-ray images from two children with the same kind of abnormality could easily be mixed up. The patterns of malformations were so complex, however, that she called the birth-defect children her "little crossword puzzles."

Wanting to learn more about these problems, Taussig traveled to Canada in 1938 to visit the world's greatest expert on congenital heart defects, a physician named Maude Abbott (1869–1940). Abbott's *Atlas of Congenital Cardiac Disease,* published in 1936, was practically the only book on this poorly understood subject. As curator of the medical museum at McGill University in Montreal, furthermore, she had assembled a huge collection of preserved specimens of malformed hearts. After speaking to Abbott and inspecting this collection, Taussig began a more modest collection of her own at Johns Hopkins.

In some ways, Taussig's increasing knowledge simply made her frustration worse. She might be able to tell which of the many kinds of heart defects her patients had, but she could do nothing to help them. No medicine could make up for the defects, and no operation could repair them. The sickly, blue-lipped children simply lived their short, restricted lives and then died.

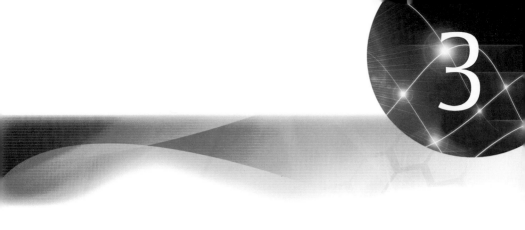

Chief of Surgery

Of all the heart-related birth defects Helen Taussig saw in her clinic, the one she encountered most often was a group of four malformations that usually occurred together. They were called *tetralogy of Fallot* (*tetra-* means "four"), after Étienne-Louis Fallot (1850–1911), a professor of forensic pathology in Marseilles, France, who described them in 1888. Because the defects kept the children's blood from obtaining as much oxygen as it needed, turning their skin cyanotic or bluish, infants who suffered from tetralogy of Fallot were often termed *blue babies*. About 75 percent of the cyanotic children who came to Taussig had tetralogy of Fallot.

A QUARTET OF DEFECTS

Human hearts are divided into four chambers. The upper two are called *atria* (singular: atrium), and the lower two, *ventricles*. A solid wall of muscle, the *septum*, separates them. In a healthy heart, bluish, oxygen-depleted blood from the body flows into the right atrium and then into the right ventricle. From there the pulmonary artery carries the blood to the lungs, where it picks up oxygen. The blood turns bright red as the oxygen binds to molecules of hemoglobin in its red cells. The blood then circles back through the *pulmonary vein* to the left atrium, from which it is pumped down to the left ventricle and then out through a huge vessel called the *aorta*. The aorta divides into many smaller vessels that carry the blood throughout the body,

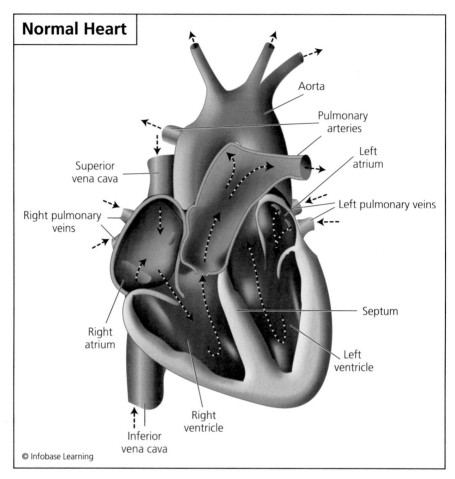

Normal Heart

Aorta

Pulmonary arteries

Left atrium

Superior vena cava

Left pulmonary veins

Right pulmonary veins

Septum

Right atrium

Left ventricle

Right ventricle

Inferior vena cava

© Infobase Learning

This diagram shows the main parts of a normal heart, seen as they would appear if one were facing the heart. A human heart has four chambers—two upper chambers called atria and two lower ones called ventricles. A solid wall of muscle, the septum, separates the right and left pairs of chambers. The body's largest blood vessels (the vena cava, the aorta, and the pulmonary arteries and veins) connect to the heart.

bringing life-giving oxygen and carrying away carbon dioxide and other waste products.

In tetralogy of Fallot, four things are wrong with this normal picture. The most important defect, Helen Taussig realized, is a severe narrowing, or *stenosis,* of the pulmonary artery, which keeps most of the child's blood from reaching its lungs. The right ventricle of the heart works harder than usual in attempting to pump blood through this narrow spot, so the ventricle becomes

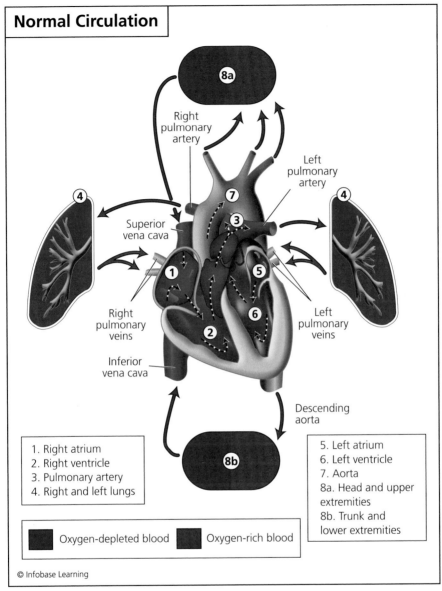

Normal Circulation

8a

Right pulmonary artery

Left pulmonary artery

4

7

3

4

Superior vena cava

1

5

Right pulmonary veins

6

Left pulmonary veins

2

Inferior vena cava

Descending aorta

1. Right atrium
2. Right ventricle
3. Pulmonary artery
4. Right and left lungs

8b

5. Left atrium
6. Left ventricle
7. Aorta
8a. Head and upper extremities
8b. Trunk and lower extremities

■ Oxygen-depleted blood   ■ Oxygen-rich blood

© Infobase Learning

This diagram shows a simplified version of the blood circulation in a normal person. Clear areas contain oxygen-enriched blood; shaded areas contain oxygen-poor blood. Oxygen-depleted blood from the body enters the right atrium through two large veins called the vena cavae (1). It then flows into the right ventricle (2), which pumps it into the pulmonary artery (3). This artery carries the blood to the lungs, where it receives oxygen (4). The blood returns to the heart through the pulmonary veins, which enter the left atrium (5). The blood flows into the left ventricle (6), which pumps it into the aorta (7). The aorta branches into many other arteries that transport the oxygen-rich blood throughout the body (8).

enlarged—a second defect. The children also have a hole in the wall of muscle that separates the right and left ventricles, which means that oxygen-poor blood from the right ventricle flows into the left ventricle and from there is pushed back into the body, adding to the oxygen deprivation caused by the narrowed pulmonary artery. Finally, the aorta in these children is further to the right than it should be, which means that it receives not only oxygen-

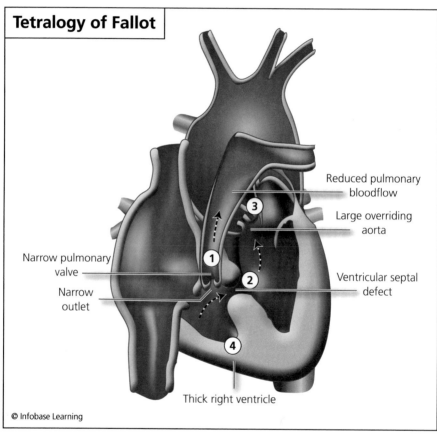

Tetralogy of Fallot

Reduced pulmonary bloodflow

Large overriding aorta

Narrow pulmonary valve

Narrow outlet

Ventricular septal defect

Thick right ventricle

© Infobase Learning

In children born with tetralogy of Fallot, the heart and nearby blood vessels have four defects. The most important is a narrow pulmonary valve and pulmonary artery, which severely limit blood flow to the lungs and thereby prevent most of the blood from picking up life-giving oxygen (1). These children also have a hole in the wall (septum) separating their right and left ventricles (2) and an aorta placed further to the right than normal (3). Both of these defects allow oxygen-rich and oxygen-poor blood to mix, which they would not normally do, and mean that the aorta (and therefore the body) receives this mixture instead of the oxygen-rich blood it would normally carry. The right ventricle of the heart pumps harder than usual in an attempt to push blood into the narrowed pulmonary artery, so the ventricle wall thickens (4).

containing blood from the left ventricle but also oxygen-depleted blood from the right ventricle.

The lack of oxygen in children with "tet," as the condition was called for short, caused far more serious problems than a blue skin color. Tet children gasped for air and often collapsed if they tried the slightest exercise. Older children spent much of their time in a squatting position, which seemed to help them breathe. When they had severe "tet spells," they might lose consciousness for 30 minutes or longer. They also often had clubbed fingers and toes and an abnormally high number of red cells in their blood; their bodies produced the extra cells in an attempt to obtain more oxygen. Helen Taussig was the first to recognize that lack of oxygen, not heart failure, was the root problem that made most children with tetralogy of Fallot die at an early age.

CLOSING AND OPENING

There was no treatment, surgical or otherwise, for tetralogy of Fallot. In 1939, however, Taussig heard about a new operation for a different birth defect that made her think. The defect was called a *patent,* or open, *ductus arteriosus.* It arose when a condition that was normal in unborn babies did not change after birth.

Before a baby is born, it does not use its lungs. The bloodstream of the fetus, or unborn child, is connected to its mother's circulation, and the mother's blood provides all the oxygen that the fetus needs. The fetus's pulmonary artery thus does not need to carry blood from the heart to the lungs, as it does after birth. Instead, this artery connects directly to the aorta by means of an extra little vessel, or shunt, termed the ductus arteriosus. This transports most of the blood from the pulmonary artery to the body rather than the lungs.

The ductus arteriosus is no longer needed after birth, and it normally closes within a few months. In a small number of children, however, the ductus fails to close on schedule. This open ductus takes blood away from the main body circulation, which stunts the children's growth. The defect also greatly increases the children's risk of developing infections in their hearts or suffering heart failure. Few children with a patent ductus lived beyond their 20s.

In 1938, Robert Gross (1905–88), a Boston surgeon, performed a daring operation in which he sewed shut a ductus arteriosus that had failed to close on its own. When Helen Taussig heard about the new procedure, she remembered that she had encountered a few children with both a patent ductus arteriosus and tetralogy of Fallot. Strange as it might seem, these children

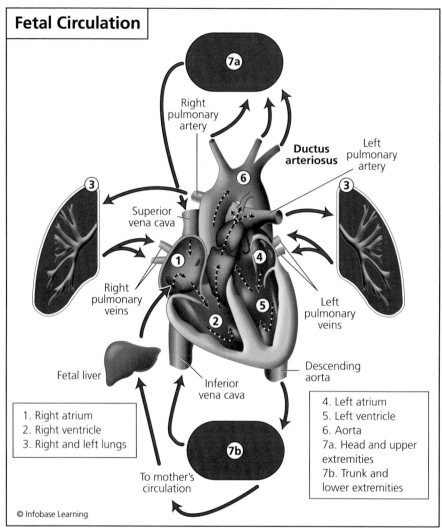

Fetal Circulation

1. Right atrium
2. Right ventricle
3. Right and left lungs

4. Left atrium
5. Left ventricle
6. Aorta
7a. Head and upper extremities
7b. Trunk and lower extremities

© Infobase Learning

A fetus, or unborn baby, does not use its lungs before birth, so most of the blood in its pulmonary artery bypasses the lungs and flows directly into the aorta. The blood is transferred through a small vessel, or shunt, called the ductus arteriosus, which is shown in this diagram of the unborn child's circulation. The ductus arteriosus normally seals off soon after birth, after which all the blood from the pulmonary artery goes to the lungs.

were less ill than children who had "tet" alone. Furthermore, if the ductus in such children either closed belatedly on its own or was closed through surgery, they became bluer and weaker. It occurred to Taussig that while the ductus arteriosus was open, it kept the children fairly healthy because it let blood reach their lungs by a route that bypassed their narrowed pulmonary arteries. If an open ductus could be closed by surgery, she thought, perhaps surgeons could also open—or create—a ductus where a natural one no longer existed. Such a procedure could be a lifesaver for children with tetralogy of Fallot.

Taussig traveled to Boston around 1940 and proposed her idea to Gross, but the now-famous surgeon was not interested. Laughing at herself decades later, Taussig said ruefully, "Dr. Gross was in [the] full flush of saying how wonderful it was to tie off the ductus. It seemed pretty foolish to him to have me suggest he put a ductus in again. I think he thought it was one of the craziest things he'd heard in a long time." Judson G. Randolph, a surgeon who knew Gross, remembered the visit this way in William S. Stoney's *Pioneers of Cardiac Surgery*:

> [Taussig] just laid it out for Dr. Gross. . . . She said, "Dr. Gross, in these blue babies, if you could just put an artery into the pulmonary artery, and if we could perfuse blood that way into the lung system, we would save a lot of children's lives." Dr. Gross didn't get it. I will never understand why. . . . For years Dr. Gross used to kick himself for not grasping that opportunity.

Unable to find a surgeon bold enough to try her plan, Taussig put it on her mental back burner and went back to diagnosing and treating her "little crossword puzzles" (as she is quoted as calling them in the chapter about her in Sherwin Nuland's book about famous physicians, *Doctors: The Biography of Medicine*) as best she could. She paid little attention at first to a piece of news she heard in early 1941, because it did not seem to affect her: The Johns Hopkins Hospital was about to have a new chief of surgery. His name was Alfred Blalock.

A FATEFUL DECISION

Alfred Blalock was not Johns Hopkins's first choice for chief surgeon, but he had much to recommend him. Although he was only 41 years old, his shock experiments had made him famous in the surgical community. Hopkins president Isaiah Bowman (1878–1950) offered Blalock the post in December 1940.

The chance to fill such a high position at the medical school he had always loved was a dream come true for Blalock, even though he would earn less money at Hopkins than at Vanderbilt. Nonetheless, he made the same condition to Hopkins that he had done to the Ford hospital in 1937: He would

ROBERT E. GROSS (1905–1988): PIONEERING CHILDREN'S HEART SURGEON

Robert Edward Gross was a contemporary of Alfred Blalock, Helen Taussig, and Vivien Thomas, and his career had features in common with all of theirs. Like Blalock, Gross was a pioneering surgeon of the heart and blood vessels; like Taussig, he was a specialist in the diseases of children; and like Thomas, he was an excellent mechanic.

Gross was born in Baltimore on July 2, 1905, and grew up there. He studied chemistry at Carleton College in Northfield, Minnesota, graduating in 1927. Shortly afterward, a biography of renowned 19th-century Canadian surgeon Sir William Osler (1849–1919) by an equally famous living surgeon Harvey Cushing (1869–1939) inspired him to turn from chemistry to medicine. He went to Harvard Medical School to study under Cushing and earned his M.D. in 1931.

In 1938, Gross became chief resident in surgery at Children's Hospital in Boston. His supervisor was William E. Ladd (1880–1967), the hospital's chief of surgery. Gross and a pediatrician colleague, John Hubbard, developed an operation for closing a ductus arteriosus in the laboratory. The cautious Ladd thought the operation was not yet ready to try on humans, but Gross disagreed.

Before Ladd left for his vacation in August 1938, he warned Gross, "Whatever you do, don't operate on that little girl [a patient in the hospital] with the patent ductus." As soon as Ladd was gone, however, Gross did precisely that. On August 26, 1938, he tied shut the open ductus of the seven-year-old girl. She not only survived but was reported to still be in "excellent health" at age 76 in 2007. After Gross presented a paper on his operation to the American Surgical Association in 1939, another surgeon at the meeting Mont. R. Reid said, "There can be no doubt that you have made an enduring contribution to the knowledge and art of surgery."

Gross went on to pioneer many other heart and blood vessel procedures and devices, including surgical correction of another birth defect, *coarctation* (narrowing) of the aorta, and a *heart-lung machine* small enough to be used on babies. (A heart-lung machine takes over the functions of those organs temporarily during heart surgery. It keeps the body supplied with oxygen, allowing the heart to be stopped so the surgeon can work on it more easily.) He and Ladd also wrote a classic textbook, *Abdominal Surgery of Infancy and Childhood*, which was published in 1941 and extensively revised in 1953.

Gross was chief surgeon at Children's Hospital from 1947 to 1966, after which he became director of the hospital's cardiac research program. Among many other honors, he received the Albert Lasker Award (along with Blalock and Taussig) in 1954; he went on to win the award again in 1959, becoming the only physician to receive it twice. Gross died of Alzheimer's disease on October 11, 1988.

Boston surgeon Robert E. Gross (1905–88) developed an operation for closing a patent, or open, ductus arteriosus in 1938. This operation, only one of Gross's contributions to surgery, gave Helen Taussig the idea of creating an artificial ductus to send more blood to the lungs of children with tetralogy of Fallot. *(National Library of Medicine)*

accept the job only if he could bring Vivien Thomas with him. Hopkins was by no means free of racial prejudice, but it did hire African Americans, so it agreed to Blalock's demand.

Blalock quickly learned, however, that winning over Johns Hopkins was only part of his task. Thomas, as always, was his own man, and the fact that Blalock had arranged a position for him did not automatically mean that he would accept it. Before deciding, Thomas wanted to discuss the matter with his wife, Clara.

The Great Depression had begun to ease by this time, and construction jobs were once again plentiful in Nashville. Thomas felt sure he would have no trouble finding carpentry work if he stayed in that city. On the other hand, he now truly enjoyed working in the laboratory, and his prospects in that line without Blalock were much less encouraging. Barney Brooks had told him that there would be "no place" for him in the Vanderbilt laboratories if Blalock left, and Nashville had no other medical research laboratory that was likely to equal Blalock's. Therefore, Thomas wrote later, "If I wanted to stay in the [research] field, it meant we would have to move to Baltimore."

Another factor the Thomases had to consider was the dark cloud of war then threatening to engulf the world. Germany, under the Nazi regime of Adolf Hitler, had taken over much of continental Europe and was attacking the remaining free European countries, including Britain. Japan was expanding its empire among the territories and islands of Southeast Asia. The United States had not yet entered the war, but most citizens believed that it would do so soon, and young men were already being drafted into the military. Thomas was exempt for the time being because he had two young children, but if war came, that might not be enough. Thomas reasoned that if he was drafted, having a position with the prestigious Johns Hopkins medical school would make it more likely that he would serve in a medical unit, which he preferred.

Taking all these factors into account, the Thomases decided that they "didn't have much to lose" by giving Baltimore a try. If they did not like life there, they agreed, they would return to Nashville. With that possibility in mind, they rented out their home in that city rather than selling it.

CHALLENGING STEREOTYPES

Vivien Thomas arrived in Baltimore on June 20, 1941, a few days ahead of Alfred Blalock. Blalock had already bought a house for his family during an earlier visit, but Thomas had no such luck. Baltimore was booming as defense industries expanded and people poured in to take advantage of the resulting jobs, so available homes were scarce. Finding housing was especially hard for African Americans, who were barred from many locations. The apartment that Thomas finally obtained was at the edge of what he considered tolerable. Fortunately, he and his family located a better one a few months later.

The day after Blalock arrived, he gave Thomas a tour of his beloved school. Thomas found some of its buildings impressive but was dismayed to see the city pressing so close to them, a far cry from the "spacious, tree-lined campus" of Vanderbilt. Even more distressing were the research laboratories, housed in a gloomy structure called the old Hunterian building (because a newer building, used for a different purpose, had been given the same name)—or, less formally, the "dog house." Thomas recalled later that he "was not quite prepared for either the age or odor of the laboratory building." Its dingy tile floors and hospital-green walls swarmed with cockroaches, especially at night. Thomas repainted the walls of the laboratory assigned to him and Blalock a light gray in the hope of brightening it a little.

Thomas soon had other issues to consider besides the laboratory's appearance. The assistants who already worked there were cooperative enough, but they were astounded when he told them that he, not Blalock, would be doing most of the operations on the dogs involved in their research. Their amazement made Thomas realize that his position as a person (and an African American at that) without an academic degree doing advanced research work was unique, certainly at Hopkins and perhaps in the country. He realized that not everyone would recognize or appreciate his unusual status.

People outside the laboratory sometimes reacted even more strongly to Thomas than the assistants. Unlike the more convenient arrangement in Nashville, where Blalock's office and laboratory were next to each other, Blalock's office at Johns Hopkins was more than a block away from the old Hunterian building. One day several months after their arrival, Blalock called Thomas at the laboratory and asked him to bring some papers to the office. Without bothering to change out of his white laboratory coat, Thomas complied. As he hurried along the endless corridor that connected all the medical buildings, he noticed that he was leaving a trail of scowls and open-mouthed stares behind him. Finally he realized why: No one at the medical school had ever seen a black man wearing a lab coat. Such a coat suggested a professional position, and they could not imagine an African American

People in the Johns Hopkins facilities, still mostly segregated in the 1940s, were startled to see Vivien Thomas wearing his white laboratory coat, as shown here. They could not imagine an African American holding the kind of professional position that the coat implied. *(Alan Mason Chesney Medical Archives of the Johns Hopkins Medical Institutions)*

holding that kind of job. After that, Thomas changed into a suit before he went to Blalock's office.

Thomas found that Baltimore in general and Johns Hopkins in particular showed much more obvious prejudice against African Americans than he had encountered in Nashville. In Baltimore department stores, for instance, African Americans could try on hats only if they put a piece of paper between their heads and the hats. Signs of segregation were everywhere at Hopkins. Several of the wards and clinics were segregated, and so were many other facilities, such as waiting rooms and restrooms. Even death did not end segregation: White and African-American corpses had separate refrigerators in the hospital morgue. Most African Americans on the Hopkins payroll did cleaning duties, and the university had a citywide reputation for paying them poorly. Thomas was the only one of his race who worked in the laboratory.

As at Vanderbilt, Thomas felt that he, and African Americans in general, had more to lose than to gain by bringing up racial discrimination. Thomas knew he was "something of a curiosity or an oddity around Hopkins," as he delicately put it, and he did not want to attract additional attention to himself. When the questions of a reporter for an African-American newspaper who interviewed him in December 1941 suggested that the reporter's article would have a racial slant, Thomas "told him that I did not consider my position a racial issue. . . . If I delivered [that is, did good work], they [the Hopkins administrators] couldn't use me as an excuse to not hire Negroes in any capacity. If he insisted on making a headline story about me being here, they might think about it and form a policy. I told him to just keep me out of his newspaper."

Alfred Blalock also had trouble fitting in at Johns Hopkins in the first months after he assumed his duties as the Hopkins hospital's chief of surgery on July 1, 1941. (He was also a full professor of surgery at the medical school and chairman of its surgery department.) In spite of the high reputation his shock experiments had earned, some of the hospital staff felt that he was too young for the post, and others thought he was just a "laboratory surgeon," lacking in hospital experience. Blalock had also made enemies by announcing that he planned to make sweeping changes in the hospital's training program for surgeons. The entire senior house staff wrote and signed a letter of protest against his policies, which they presented to him in late 1941. Mary Blalock said later that she had never seen her husband so angry. Only after several encounters with the famous Blalock temper did the staff come to realize that, young though he might be, the new chief surgeon demanded respect. As they came to know him better, they realized that he was worthy of it as well.

CRUSH SYNDROME

With World War II looming in the future, Blalock's continuing research on shock was more important than ever. The National Research Council had appointed him to its committee on surgery and made him chairman of a subcommittee on shock in 1939, and in 1940, Blalock's book on shock, *Principles of Surgical Care: Shock and Other Problems,* appeared. This work was a standard textbook on shock for many years.

Around this time, while he was still at Vanderbilt, Blalock also began a series of experiments on a related problem called *crush syndrome.* This condition affected people who were trapped under piles of rubble for hours before being rescued, as often happened when falling bombs destroyed homes and other buildings. Such people seemed to do well at first if their injuries were not too severe, but several hours after their rescue, they sometimes went into shock. They might also develop kidney failure, which could be fatal. No one knew the reason for this delayed reaction.

Blalock continued his experiments at Johns Hopkins—or rather, Vivien Thomas and George Duncan, a medical student who had come with Blalock and Thomas from Vanderbilt, continued them. Blalock's duties at the hospital and medical school left him time for only one or two brief visits to the laboratory each week. He outlined what he hoped to accomplish, then Thomas and Duncan did their best to make it happen.

As with shock, the first step in understanding the cause of crush syndrome and looking for a treatment for the condition was finding a way to imitate the condition in animals. Duncan invented a device that could crush the muscle of an anesthetized dog's thigh without damaging the leg bone. The device also cut off blood circulation in the leg, much as a heap of bricks or plaster pressing on a person's leg might do. After Duncan and Thomas left the instrument on an animal's leg for five hours and then removed it, the leg swelled, and shock developed. Some dogs showed signs of kidney trouble as well. Most of the animals injured in this way died.

Blalock's experiments at Vanderbilt had shown that toxins did not cause the shock that resulted from simple muscle injury. Some of Thomas and Duncan's experiments revealed, however, that the shock produced by crush syndrome was different. Several hours after dogs' legs had been released from the compression device, the researchers collected lymph (a clear fluid that circulates through the body and carries immune cells and chemicals) from the animals and injected it into smaller dogs. The lymph made the dogs' blood pressure drop and produced signs of kidney failure in about half of them. A quarter of the dogs died. These results suggested that the crushing had produced a toxic substance in the lymph.

The two men next tested possible treatments for crush syndrome. The best one, they found, was a pneumatic cuff or boot. By putting gentle pressure on the injured limb, the device kept blood pressure in the limb from falling and reduced the amount of swelling. About three-fourths of the animals treated in this way survived. The cuffs and boots had little effect on the kidney failure problem, however.

By this time, the threatened war had arrived. The United States entered World War II on December 7, 1941, after Japan staged a surprise aerial bombing attack on the U.S. military base at Pearl Harbor, Hawaii. Most of the male medical students, surgeons in training, and hospital staff departed soon afterward for military service. Left with only a skeleton staff to care for his patients, Blalock was busier than ever. Most of his research plans, it seemed, would have to wait for more peaceful times.

Blue Babies

As many a judge and jury have discovered, different people's memories of the same events can vary widely. This is especially true when the event is one that arouses strong emotions, such as a violent crime—or a key moment in a major scientific discovery. So it has proved to be regarding the development of what came to be called the blue baby operation. After the operation became famous around the world, Helen Taussig, Alfred Blalock, and to some extent Vivien Thomas (and their respective supporters and biographers) all told different stories about exactly who had thought of what. As Mark Ravitch wrote regarding this issue (in the introduction to Vivien Thomas's autobiography), "It is apparent to most historians that historical truth is difficult to arrive at, and in fact may not exist."

A NEW OPERATION

Perhaps as an outgrowth of the blood vessel connection experiments that he and Thomas had done at Vanderbilt, Alfred Blalock began to develop an interest in heart surgery about the time he came to Johns Hopkins. In those days, this field hardly existed. A few surgeons, including Blalock himself, had repaired bullet or stab wounds in the *pericardium,* or even the heart itself, and pioneers like Robert Gross had operated on the great blood vessels near the heart. For the most part, however, the heart was still forbidden surgical territory.

According to A. McGehee Harvey, a longtime Johns Hopkins physician who wrote a history of the Hopkins medical school and hospital, Blalock and Taussig first met in fall 1942, when Blalock performed Gross's operation to close an open ductus arteriosus. Taussig saw the operation and said, "I stand in awe and admiration of your surgical skill, but the really great day will come when you build a ductus for a child who is dying . . . and not when you tie off a ductus for a child who has a little too much blood going to the lungs." Blalock replied that such an operation would make closing a ductus "seem like child's play."

Blalock did nothing further with Taussig's idea at that time. Instead, his attention turned to another type of birth defect called coarctation of the aorta. In children born with this defect, the aorta is abnormally constricted or narrowed. The result is very high blood pressure in the arms and head, putting patients at risk of death from a stroke or a heart attack. Helen Taussig's mentor, Edwards Park, asked Blalock casually one day in spring 1943 whether he could find a way to treat coarctation surgically.

Blalock, as usual, turned to the laboratory—that is, to Vivien Thomas— for an answer to the problem. To produce an artificial defect similar to coarctation, they clamped the aorta in two places to prevent bleeding, cut the the vessel open between the two clamps, then sewed the cut ends shut. They treated the condition in a second operation by making a small opening in the part of the aorta that connected with the rest of the body and sewing the subclavian artery into the opening, which routed blood around the closed-off section of the aorta and allowed the circulation to resume. This surgery was more difficult than the end-to-end vessel connections that Thomas and Blalock had used at Vanderbilt, because the new procedure involved connecting the end of one blood vessel to the side of another.

CONFLICTING STORIES

Alfred Blalock wrote a paper describing the coarctation operation, put Edwards Park's name on it as well as his own (because Park had proposed the idea of treating coarctation surgically), and left a copy of it on Park's desk about six months after Park had brought up the subject. Park was amazed and impressed. He discussed the coarctation operation with Blalock in a meeting shortly afterward—a meeting that proved to be very important, because Helen Taussig was also present.

As Taussig recalled this meeting, Park proposed using the carotid artery, the artery in the neck that supplies blood to the head, rather than

EARLY HEART SURGERY

"Surgery of the heart has probably reached the limit set by nature to all surgery," the eminent British surgeon Stephen Paget (1855–1926) wrote in 1896. "No new method and no new discovery can overcome the natural difficulties that attend a wound of the heart."

Paget did not know that history was already proving him wrong. In 1893, three years before he made his statement, Daniel Hale Williams (1856–1931), an African-American surgeon in Chicago, had sewed up an inch-long stab wound in the pericardium. A German surgeon Ludwig Rehn sutured a wound in the heart itself in 1896, the very year in which Paget said that heart surgery was impossible. Luther L. Hill performed a similar operation in Montgomery, Alabama, in 1902—working on a kitchen table by the light of a kerosene lantern.

Surgeons had become able to remove bullets and other foreign bodies from the heart even earlier. The first such operation took place in London in 1873, and by the early 20th century, bullets could be cut out of the heart fairly dependably if they did not cause immediate death.

In spite of these limited advances and the more recent one made by Robert Gross, most surgeons in the early 1940s probably would have basically agreed with Paget. As the heart surgeon Judson G. Randolph put it in William S. Stoney's *Pioneers of Cardiac Surgery*, "The heart was a big heaving thing that everybody avoided because they couldn't get to it or do anything with it." No one realized how soon or how completely that view would change.

the subclavian artery as a bypass for coarctation. Taussig then said, "If you [can] put the carotid artery into the descending aorta [to treat coarctation], couldn't you put the subclavian artery into the pulmonary artery [to treat tetralogy of Fallot]?" "There is no question that the idea [for the blue baby operation] . . . was mine," she insisted in a 1976 interview. Edwards Park, however, told Mark Ravitch in 1965 that he remembered the meeting differently: "In my presence Dr. Taussig asked [Blalock] if he could not do something by operation to give patients with the Tetralogy of Fallot adequate pulmonary circulation . . . but without suggesting how this could be done."

Blalock agreed to take on this new problem. He asked Taussig to come to his laboratory so that Vivien Thomas could be part of their discussion about the best way to proceed. Accounts of that meeting also differ. Thomas wrote, "[Taussig] expressed her belief that, by surgical means, it should be possible to do something to get more blood to the lungs, as a plumber changes pipes around, but gave us no hint as to how this could be accomplished—what pipes to put where." Taussig, however, claimed that she told Thomas both how to produce the cyanosis that the "tet" children suffered and how to treat it. "I suggested that he put the right pulmonary artery into the left auricle [old term for atrium]—that's going to pull venous blood into the systemic [body] circulation and will produce cyanosis. Then put the subclavian artery into the pulmonary artery, and see if you relieve it."

Since Taussig had already spoken to Robert Gross about building an artificial ductus arteriosus, it seems likely that she had a fairly precise idea of the kind of operation she wanted by the time she talked to Blalock. On the other hand, Blalock may well have been the one who decided which blood vessels to connect—because he and Thomas had already done it in 1938 as part of their failed attempt to create high blood pressure in the lungs. The two apparently realized almost immediately that this same operation, in which the subclavian artery was joined to the pulmonary artery, potentially could help Taussig's blue babies. In an interview with the medical historian Peter Olch in 1967, Vivian Thomas said, "The Professor [Blalock] and I just looked at each other [when Taussig brought up the possibility of treating tetralogy of Fallot with a surgical bypass]. We knew we had the answer in the Vanderbilt work."

In any case, as Blalock later pointed out, having an idea is only the first step in turning that idea into reality. "If I make the statement to you that you could improve the condition of patients with aortic stenosis if you could find a means to allow more [oxygen-rich] blood to reach the body, . . . I would be far from solving the practical problem," Blalock stated in a letter in September 1945.

MAKING IT HAPPEN

Whoever proposed the idea of the blue baby operation, the job of making it happen fell largely to Vivien Thomas. He and Blalock already knew how to perform the surgery itself, but to learn whether it would help children with tetralogy of Fallot, he first had to re-create that condition, or something like it, in his laboratory dogs. This proved to be the hardest part of the research project. Thomas recognized that the combination of four heart and blood vessel defects would be too complex to reproduce, but he hoped to mimic the most important of the four, the narrowing of the pulmonary artery.

After several failed attempts, Thomas and Blalock concluded that simply narrowing or tying off the pulmonary artery was not enough to produce the severe cyanosis they wanted. They also needed to make a shunt, or connection, that allowed oxygen-depleted blood to flow back into the body without passing through the lungs, just as the hole in the "tet" children's hearts did. They found that removing part of the animals' lungs and connecting a branch of the pulmonary artery and a branch of the pulmonary vein to one another produced a circuit that served their purpose. Dogs operated on in this way developed the same blue coloration, inability to endure exercise, and thick, dark blood that the blue babies had.

Once these sick dogs were created, it was a relatively easy matter to show that the artery-joining operation Thomas and Blalock had created at Vanderbilt helped the animals by allowing more blood to reach their lungs and receive oxygen. They modified their original procedure by using the end-to-side connection that they had developed for coarctation of the aorta, in this case connecting the end of the subclavian artery to the side of the pulmonary artery, so that the blood would reach both lungs. They tried the operation first on a dog named Anna, who not only survived it but lived to see her portrait installed in the Johns Hopkins medical library in 1952. She was the only animal to receive such an honor.

Thomas tested the procedure on more than 200 dogs before Blalock considered it ready for a human trial. The task of choosing that first human patient fell to Helen Taussig. She and Blalock agreed that it should be the sickest of her "tet" children. "You don't do a new operation on a good risk," Blalock said. "You do a new operation on a patient who has no hope of survival without it."

A SICKLY BABY

The child Helen Taussig chose for that historic first operation was a scrawny baby named Eileen Saxon. Eileen had been born at Johns Hopkins on August 3, 1943. She could survive only inside an oxygen tent, and even then she frequently lost consciousness because her blood contained so little oxygen. In late November 1944, when Eileen was 15 months old, it became clear to Taussig that the child would die unless she had surgery immediately. At that

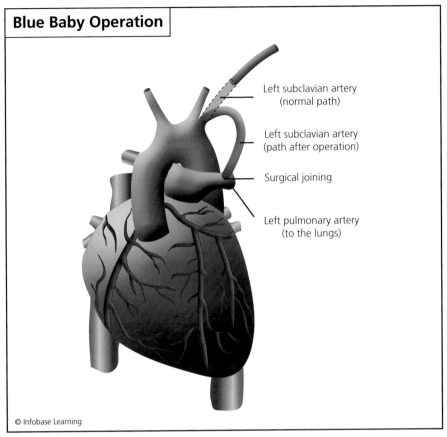

Blue Baby Operation

Left subclavian artery
(normal path)

Left subclavian artery
(path after operation)

Surgical joining

Left pulmonary artery
(to the lungs)

© Infobase Learning

In the famous blue baby operation, formally known as the Blalock-Taussig shunt, part of the subclavian artery (or sometimes another nearby artery, the innominate artery) was bent down and sewed into an opening that the surgeon made in the side of the pulmonary artery. This operation, done only on the left side, bypassed the narrow part of the pulmonary artery and allowed more blood to reach the lungs, where it could pick up oxygen.

time, Eileen weighed a mere nine pounds; she was smaller than most of the dogs Thomas had operated on.

Blalock warned Saxon's parents that she might die during the operation. William Longmire, who would be Blalock's first assistant during the operation, shared the surgeon's fears. When Longmire first saw Eileen on the night before the surgery, he wrote in William S. Stoney's *Pioneers of Cardiac Surgery,* "I took one look at [her] . . . and thought, 'My God, this man isn't going to operate on this patient.' The child was very cyanotic with dark blue lips and fingernails."

Eileen's health was not the only reason for concern. Vivien Thomas had carried out all the operations on the dogs; Blalock had observed many of the surgeries, but, for reasons known only to himself, had assisted Thomas during only one of them. Blalock had hoped to perform the blood vessel operation on a dog under Thomas's supervision before trying it on a human patient, but Eileen's worsening condition deprived him of that chance. At Taussig's urging, he agreed to operate on the baby on November 29.

Even if the concept of the operation was right, its chances of succeeding on Eileen Saxon seemed as small and fragile as the child herself. The hospital's chief of anesthesiology, Austin Lamont, doubted whether she could even survive anesthesia. Furthermore, the equipment for giving anesthesia to such a tiny baby and for sewing up her blood vessels—half the thickness of those in the dogs that had been used to develop the operation—essentially did not exist. Vivien Thomas had to bring in some of the tools he had used in the laboratory, including tiny suturing needles that he had made by cutting down standard ones.

HISTORIC SURGERY

The surgical group assembled anxiously on that fateful morning: Blalock, Longmire, anesthesiologist Merel Harmel, intern Denton Cooley, and scrub nurse Charlotte Mitchell. Helen Taussig also scrubbed up and put on surgical garments so she could stand in the operating room and observe. Vivien Thomas, on the other hand, had decided that he did not want to watch. "I might make Dr. Blalock nervous," he told the laboratory's chemistry technician, Clara Belle Puryear, the day before the operation, "—or even worse, he might make *me* nervous." Blalock, however, refused to proceed without Thomas and sent Puryear to find him.

At Blalock's insistence, Thomas put on surgical clothes and joined the group in the operating room. He stood on a stool just behind Blalock so that he could see as much as possible of what was happening to the tiny patient, who was hardly visible under the surgical drapes. Answering Blalock's periodic questions, he made sure that Blalock made incisions of the right size and sewed the almost-microscopic sutures in the correct direction. Taussig, by contrast, was silent throughout the procedure.

"The operation was one of the most difficult in which I have ever participated," William Longmire wrote in his diary six months later. He was shocked to see "thick black blood [that] . . . looked like purple molasses" ooz-

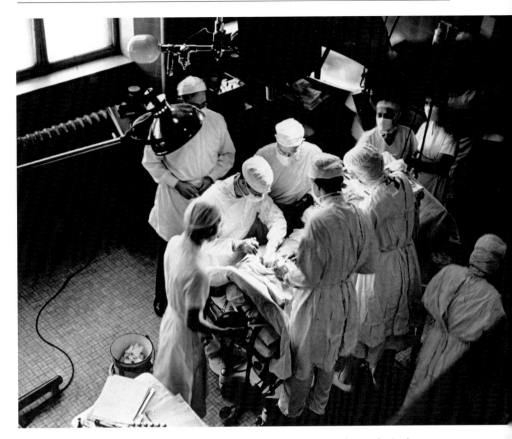

During the early blue baby surgeries, Alfred Blalock insisted that Vivien Thomas be in the operating room to advise him as he sutured the children's tiny blood vessels. Thomas is visible in the top left of this photo, standing on a stool behind Blalock. *(Alan Mason Chesney Medical Archives of the Johns Hopkins Medical Institutions)*

ing from Eileen's blood vessels as Blalock made his first incision, a sight very different from the spurting drops of red that he would have observed in a healthy child.

The team held their breath when, an hour and a half after the fragile baby had been wheeled into the operating room, the clamps holding her arteries shut were finally removed. If Blalock's stitches did not hold, blood could spurt out, and Eileen would quickly bleed to death. They did hold, however—almost no bleeding occurred—and the child's blue lips suddenly turned pink. "You've never seen anything so dramatic," Vivien Thomas told Peter Olch many years later. Eileen's mother echoed Thomas's amazement when she spoke to medical writer Jürgen Thorwald in 1970: "When I was allowed to see Eileen for the first time, it was like a miracle. . . . I was beside myself with happiness."

Eileen had a difficult time during the next several weeks, but her condition slowly improved. On January 25, 1945, about two months after the surgery, Taussig agreed that she was well enough to go home. A few weeks later, Blalock repeated the operation on two older children: Barbara Rosenthal, a 12-year-old girl "blue as indigo" (a deep blue dye) according to William Longmire, and Marvin Mason, a six-year-old boy. Neither of these patients was as sick as Eileen had been, and both showed even more striking improvement after their surgery. When the surgical team saw Marvin Mason's lips turn from dark blue to bright red, Helen Taussig wrote later, "We knew we had won."

Blalock and Taussig wrote a scientific paper about these first three cases, which appeared in the *Journal of the American Medical Association* on May 19, 1945. As William S. Stoney points out in *Pioneers of Cardiac Surgery*, even the article's title—"The Surgical Treatment of Malformations of the Heart in Which There Is Pulmonary Stenosis or Pulmonary Atresia"—was revolutionary; it "proclaimed for the first time [except for the patent ductus operation, which had attracted little attention outside the surgical community] that surgery was to be the treatment for congenital heart disease."

FAME AND STRESS

The Associated Press picked up the story of the new operation—formally known as the *Blalock-Taussig shunt,* but more popularly called the blue baby operation—and spread it to newspapers around the world. As William Longmire wrote, "The entire concept made dramatic, almost tabloid-type news. Involved were disabled children, an abnormal color, and an operation on a malformed heart."

After that, "people came out of the walls," Vivien Thomas later told a reporter from the Baltimore *Sun.* Families with children suffering from tetralogy of Fallot and other congenital heart defects poured into the Johns Hopkins Hospital from all over the world. In his autobiography, Thomas wrote the following:

They came by automobile, train, and plane. Many had not communicated with the hospital, had no appointment in the clinic, and had no hotel reservations; thus the cardiac clinic was overrun with patients. . . . To these parents, this operation was their great hope; this was what they had been praying for.

Some of the families told amazing stories. One mother, for instance, had hitchhiked to Hopkins with her two-year-old child from their home in the Appalachian Mountains, several states away. A French couple said they had learned about the operation when a neighbor read a report of it in a newspaper wrapped around a present from a friend in the United States. A half-starved little boy who had suffered through the Japanese invasion of the Philippines during World War II came to the United States with the first boatload of returning soldiers and was brought straight to Taussig's clinic.

This widespread publicity brought instant fame—at least to Alfred Blalock. William Longmire wrote that Blalock was always generous in giving Taussig and others credit for their share in the development of the groundbreaking operation, but Taussig and Vivien Thomas might not have agreed. Thomas, for instance, was not mentioned at all in the *Journal of the American Medical Association* article, although in fairness to Blalock it should be said that such articles do not normally list technicians. Helen Taussig said publicly at times that she felt Blalock had not given her enough credit for her part in developing the operation. Longmire stated that these bad feelings, along with other tensions, drove a wedge between Blalock and Taussig, so that "a quite subtle distrust slowly evolved into a thinly suppressed hostility."

Not all the operations ended in success, of course. Even Helen Taussig's amazing diagnostic skills were wrong sometimes, and surgery revealed that certain children had defects that the blue baby operation could not help. Others were simply too sick to survive. One of these, unfortunately, was Eileen Saxon. She did fairly well for about eight months, but then her blue color returned and a second operation had to be performed. She died five days later.

Both Blalock and Taussig took the deaths of their little patients very much to heart. Whenever a child died after surgery, one or both often left the hospital for the day or shut themselves in their offices and refused to speak to anyone. They lost about one child in five at first—a high mortality rate, but not a surprising one given the newness of the procedure and the extremely poor health of the children who underwent it. By 1950, the death rate had dropped to less than 5 percent.

THE BIRTH OF CARDIAC SURGERY

The blue baby operation's occasional failures did nothing to stem the flood of desperate families that poured into Johns Hopkins. Alfred Blalock often had to perform two shunt operations a day in what became known as "the heart room," an exhausting schedule. Helen Taussig must have been equally tired as she examined the incoming children to determine which ones were likely to benefit from the surgery and watched over those who had already had the operation.

Vivien Thomas was also working almost full time on the project. Part of the diagnostic procedure involved measuring the gases in the children's blood to determine how much oxygen their bodies were receiving, a chemical test that only a few people in the hospital knew how to perform. With Clara Belle Puryear, Thomas carried out most of these tests, in addition to his continuing research and other laboratory duties.

Thomas had to collect blood for the tests, and children in the "tet room," a ward hastily set up for the young patients, learned to recognize him all too well. "My . . . presence on the floor would throw the entire floor into an uproar, since it meant that some patient was going to be stuck with a needle," he wrote ruefully in his autobiography. "One child would set it off, and in a few minutes every child on the floor would be crying at top voice." In an attempt to build a more trusting relationship with them, Thomas made a point of visiting the ward and talking to the youngsters on days when no blood samples were needed.

Thomas also had to attend most of the operations, at least at first; Blalock would have it no other way. If anyone stepped into the spot where Thomas normally stood, looking over Blalock's right shoulder, the surgeon would snap, "Only Vivien is to stand there."

During the ten years or so after its invention, the blue baby operation saved the lives of about 12,000 children—but its importance reached far beyond that. In *Pioneers of Cardiac Surgery,* William Longmire explained what the operation really meant:

> Even though the Blue Baby operation was an extracardiac procedure [one that did not involve the heart], it . . . seem[s] to be the stimulus that marks the real beginning of cardiac surgery. The repair of coarctation and closure of a patent ductus . . . preceded the Blue Baby operation, but these had not caught the interest of the surgical world.

Denton Cooley put the same idea more pithily. He called the operation "the dawn of heart surgery."

Royal Progress

The end of World War II in 1945 came none too soon for Alfred Blalock, Helen Taussig, Vivien Thomas, and the rest of the overworked staff at Johns Hopkins Hospital. They eagerly welcomed back Mark Ravitch and the many other talented surgeons and staff members who had gone overseas.

A SURGICAL POWER

By this time, thanks partly to the fame brought by the blue baby operation, Alfred Blalock had become a power to be reckoned with, not only at Johns Hopkins but in the entire surgical world. He was a regent of the American College of Surgeons and a member of the National Research Council. In June 1945, he was made a member of the National Academy of Sciences, a great honor (Taussig was also made a member, but not until much later), and elected president of the Baltimore City Medical Society, an important local position.

Other universities were well aware of Blalock's reputation. In December 1945, Columbia University in New York City invited him to become chairman of their medical school's department of surgery—at a considerably higher salary than he was receiving at Hopkins. "If we go there we will have plenty of money for the laboratory and can do all the research we want to," Blalock told Thomas, clearly assuming that both Columbia and Thomas would agree to Thomas making the move along with him if he decided to go.

After a month of hard thought, however, Blalock rejected Columbia's offer because he felt that Johns Hopkins needed him more than Columbia did. By now he was playing a major role in the administration of the Hopkins medical school and hospital, and he believed that much work needed to be done there. The institution needed more money, new facilities, and, in his opinion, a complete reorganization of its surgical staff. Around 1946, for instance, Blalock began hiring full-time surgeons in such specialties as plastic surgery (surgery involving the skin and superficial tissues) and neurosurgery (surgery involving the brain and nervous system).

Above all, Blalock focused on developing the careers of young surgeons through the hospital's internship and residency program. He wanted to hire young men who would really "do things" in surgery and was always looking for the "exceptional fellow." (He did mean *men*. Despite the medical school's policy of equality for women students, Blalock did not favor women surgeons. During his tenure as chief of surgery, the hospital accepted only one female intern, Rowena Spencer, and no female residents.)

Blalock chose well, trained well, and nurtured the careers of "his boys"—as he termed his 45 surgical residents—throughout their lives. "I had been told . . . before I went to Hopkins, that if Dr. Blalock is interested in you, he will never forget you. This proved to be very true," William H. Muller, one of Blalock's former residents, told William Longmire. Blalock's protegés, in turn, revered him and did everything they could to please him.

Thanks to both their own talent and their chief's support, almost all of Blalock's surgical residents went on to become chiefs of surgery in major hospitals, chairmen of surgical departments in university medical schools, or highly regarded surgeons in private practice. Many also became pioneers of heart surgery. "Blalock's greatest accomplishment may not be the 'Blue Baby' operation, but rather the living surgical legacy that he passed on to so many surgeons through his residents who became surgical teachers," James M. McGreevy wrote in an article about Blalock in the March–April 2003 edition of *Current Surgery*.

(opposite page) Alfred Blalock chose his chief residents in surgery carefully and nurtured their careers all his life. The combination of their own talent and his help led most of them to attain high positions in university hospitals and medical schools. This map shows some locations at which former Blalock residents became surgery department chairs or division chiefs.

Blalock School of Surgery

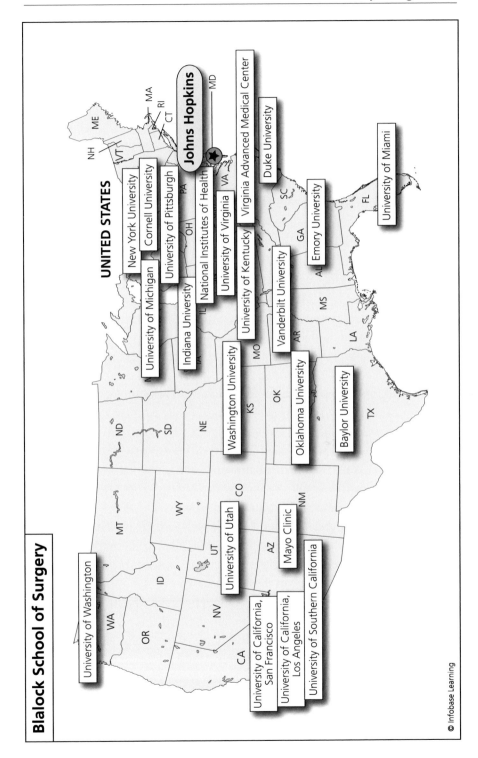

UNITED STATES

Johns Hopkins

University of Washington

University of California, San Francisco

University of California, Los Angeles

University of Southern California

University of Utah

Mayo Clinic

Baylor University

Oklahoma University

Washington University

Vanderbilt University

Indiana University

University of Michigan

National Institutes of Health

University of Virginia

University of Kentucky

Virginia Advanced Medical Center

Duke University

Emory University

University of Miami

New York University

Cornell University

University of Pittsburgh

WA
OR
ID
MT
ND
SD
NE
WY
CA
NV
UT
CO
AZ
NM
KS
OK
TX
MO
AR
LA
MS
AL
GA
FL
SC
TN
KY
IN
IL
OH
PA
VA
MD
NH
ME
VT
MA
RI
CT

© Infobase Learning

SIGNS OF STRAIN

Meanwhile, the stream of blue babies went on. Especially during the first years of the famous operation, the atmosphere in the "heart room" was often tense, and no one showed the stress more plainly than Blalock himself. His behavior in the operating room became famous—or infamous—among those who worked with him. If an operation was going badly, he said in what was universally described as a whine, "Won't somebody help me?" or "Must I operate all alone?" In fact he had a very competent and helpful surgical staff, but he told Henry Bahnson, one of his favorite residents, that "somehow it helped him to complain." Blalock's attitude upset some people who were not familiar with it, but his regular crews, aware of the real skill that underlay his childish griping, simply ignored it.

At Johns Hopkins, treating children with defective hearts meant working with Helen Taussig—and cooperation was often hard for both Blalock and Taussig. These two talented people were too much alike not to clash. Each was usually mild-mannered: Blalock was often described as the perfect Southern gentleman, and Taussig could appear to be an equally ideal New England grandmother. Both were famous for the gentleness with which they spoke to and examined their young patients. (In true Southern style, Blalock always called the little girls "sugar.") Nonetheless, both knew their strength and could explode in a fiery burst of temper if they felt that their authority was challenged. Mark Ravitch said that Blalock was "sure of his prerogatives and jealous of them," and Taussig's students did not call her "the Queen" for nothing. Blalock once told Henry Bahnson that he, Blalock, "would deserve a star in heaven for being able to work with Taussig," and Taussig probably would have laid similar claim to a star of her own.

Many of the disputes between Blalock and Taussig arose because they cared so deeply about the children they treated. Each was sure that he or she knew exactly what was best for a particular little patient, but their opinions did not always agree—and when they did not, there was bound to be trouble. Taussig seldom questioned Blalock's judgment inside the operating room, but once the children left it, she felt that she and the pediatricians who worked under her should have complete charge of their care. "They were like mother hens who felt these little chicks were theirs," Denton Cooley recalled. Blalock, in turn, wanted Taussig and her staff "out of his hair."

Cooley, the junior member of the team who had operated on Eileen Saxon, said later that Blalock chose him to head the hospital's heart service just after Cooley had completed his internship and became a junior assistant resident—an unprecedentedly rapid advance—at least partly because of this very conflict. Blalock told Cooley that he was giving him the post primarily because Cooley had the reputation of being able to handle women. "I want you to get all those women off my neck," Blalock told the young man.

Cooley, who became lifelong friends with Taussig as well as Blalock, was happy to accept the task. He told Joyce Baldwin that he had handled Taussig "just by sort of being nice and bringing her along, and making her think [that whatever he wanted her to do] was her idea." He used this sort of diplomacy, for instance, to persuade her to let him operate on children as young as three or four weeks old.

"SOMETHING THE LORD MADE"

Vivien Thomas was quite happy to stay out of the conflicts between Blalock and Taussig. In late 1945, Blalock hired Richard J. Bing to set up a cardiac physiology laboratory and take over the blood gas studies, freeing Thomas to return to full-time research. The first major project that Blalock assigned to Thomas after the blue baby operation was *transposition of the great vessels,* the most important birth defect of the heart for which there was still no treatment.

In children with this defect, the points of origin of the aorta and the pulmonary artery are reversed: the aorta arises from the right ventricle, which receives unoxygenated blood from the body, and the pulmonary artery, which normally goes from the right ventricle to the lungs, arises from the left ventricle instead. When it existed by itself, this defect was fatal, because it left the blood with no way to obtain oxygen. Most children born with transposition, however, also had one or more holes in the central wall of their hearts, so their oxygen-depleted blood mixed with oxygenated blood. The more mixing took place, the longer such a child was likely to live.

Blalock and Thomas looked for surgical ways to increase this mixing. They first tried connecting the right pulmonary vein, which carries oxygenated blood from the lungs, directly to the right atrium, but this procedure was not successful; scar tissue formed around the incision where the two were joined, shrinking the opening until it was useless. During one of these operations, however, Thomas realized that he could achieve the same effect by cutting out a small piece of the wall dividing the two upper chambers of the heart. This artificial defect, like the natural one that some children had, would allow the blood in the two chambers to mix and the pulmonary vein to flow into both. One day in 1946 he persuaded Rowena Spencer, then a medical student assisting him in the laboratory, to help him try that procedure.

Thomas's inspiration succeeded: The dog on which he and Spencer operated not only survived the surgery but was still alive and healthy looking the next morning. The two performed the surgery on six more dogs, carefully scheduling the operations for times when they knew Blalock was not likely to visit the laboratory. Thomas did not want to show Blalock his work until the dogs had survived long enough to heal completely.

All seven dogs did well, so finally, several weeks after the first operation, Thomas told Blalock what he had done. "Let's autopsy one [of the operated dogs]," Blalock said. Thomas put to sleep the first dog he had operated on, then cut out its heart and lungs and brought them to Blalock. When Blalock opened the dog's heart and examined the spot on which Thomas had operated, he found that the wound had healed so cleanly that Thomas's stitching could no longer be seen. "Vivien, are you sure you did this?" Blalock asked. When Thomas confirmed that he had, Blalock said in awe, "Well, this looks like something the Lord made"—in other words, the site looked as if it had never been altered by a human hand.

Shortly afterward, in the fall of 1946, C. Rollins Hanlon, a Hopkins resident who was interested in research, joined the laboratory. He and Thomas continued to work on the transposition operation, and Hanlon made an improvement in Thomas's procedure. Hanlon later pleased Thomas by putting Thomas's name on one of the papers that resulted from some of their other laboratory work—something that Blalock and most of the other researchers who benefited from Thomas's help did not bother to do—but Thomas said that his name should have been on the paper describing the transposition operation as well. "There is no question in my mind that Vivien is the one who invented the atrial septectomy operation, the [so-called] Blalock-Hanlon procedure," Denton Cooley wrote in William S. Stoney's *Pioneers of Cardiac Surgery*. In her *Washingtonian* article about Thomas, Katie McCabe says that this operation was "the first and only one conceived entirely by Thomas." Blalock first performed the surgery on a human in May 1948.

TENSE NEGOTIATIONS

The dispute over research credit was not the only reason why there might have been some tension between Vivien Thomas and Rollins Hanlon. Since shortly after Thomas's arrival at Hopkins, he had been in charge of the "dog

ANIMALS IN RESEARCH

The blue baby operation, the operation for transposition of the great vessels, and all the other surgeries invented by Alfred Blalock, Vivien Thomas, and others in the 1940s were perfected and tested on animals (usually dogs) before being tried on humans. This is still true of both surgical procedures and drugs.

Then and now, activists called *antivivisectionists* have protested that experimentation on animals should be forbidden because it is cruel. (Vivisection means cutting open a living thing while it is still alive.) In recent years, they have also claimed that, especially in the case of drugs, it is useless because animals' bodies are not exactly the same as those of humans. A drug that does not harm animals therefore might still be dangerous to people, or vice versa.

Both Blalock and Helen Taussig, as well as other members of the Johns Hopkins staff, spoke out against the antivivisectionists. In 1949, for instance, an antivivisectionist group came close to persuading the Baltimore city council to ban the use of stray dogs in experimentation. Taussig went to the council meeting with a group of pink-cheeked children—former blue babies who, she pointed out, owed their lives and health to the experiments on dogs that Blalock and Thomas had performed. The council sided with the researchers. Furthermore, when the antivivisectionists put a proposed law banning animal experimentation on the ballot of the next city election, more than 80 percent of the voters rejected it.

Arguments about animal experimentation still continue. Modern antivivisectionists would reject Taussig's argument because they say it is speciesist to value human lives more highly than those of animals. Most biomedical scientists feel that some experimentation on animals is necessary, but many also support what have come to be called the "three Rs": replace (substituting tests that do not involve animals, such as computer simulations, for animal tests), reduce (use fewer animals per test), and refine (redesign experiments to cause less pain to the animals). A number of organizations and research groups are working to develop alternatives that will reduce or even perhaps end experimentation on animals without limiting biomedical advances.

house" in all but name—and, of course, salary. He hired and supervised its staff, ordered its laboratory supplies and drugs, and oversaw the care of the dogs in its kennel. When Hanlon joined the laboratory, however, Blalock gave him the post of laboratory director. Thomas retained the title of "director of personnel."

At first Hanlon tried to check all of Thomas's work, but he backed off after Thomas objected, and arrangements continued very much as they had been before. "There was no doubt in anybody's mind as to who was in charge" of the laboratory, Alex Haller, an eminent surgeon who worked with both Blalock and Thomas during his years as a Hopkins resident, told Katie McCabe. "Technically, a non-M.D. could not hold the position of laboratory supervisor. Dr. Blalock always had someone on the surgical staff nominally in charge, but it was Vivien who ran the place."

Hanlon's being given the title of laboratory director may have irritated Thomas, but that seems not to have been the main factor that pushed him into making a potentially fateful decision. In November 1946, just as he had done so many years before at Vanderbilt, Thomas informed Blalock—to the latter's amazement—that he was planning to go back to being a construction carpenter in Nashville.

The reason Thomas gave for this change, just as at Vanderbilt, was money. His salary, high for a mere "technician" though it now was, was not enough to send his two daughters to college, and he was determined that they would have the education he had been forced to forgo. He believed that he could make at least twice as much money as a construction worker as he was making at Hopkins. In Nashville he also would not have to pay rent, as he did in Baltimore, because he and Clara still owned a house there.

Once again, Blalock said little in reply to Thomas's announcement. Clearly as determined to keep his valuable assistant as ever, though, he took the matter to the Hopkins administration. Over the next month, he made two salary offers, each better than the last, but not, in Thomas's opinion, good enough. Finally, just before Christmas, Blalock told Thomas that Johns Hopkins was willing to offer him an unprecedented raise, amounting to about twice what he presently made. Thomas accepted, thereby becoming the highest-paid technician, and by far the highest-paid African American, at Johns Hopkins.

Thomas still felt restless, though. In late 1947, at the age of 37 and for the first time in more than a decade, he gave serious thought to going back to college. He applied to Morgan State University, an African-American college in Baltimore. Morgan, however, refused to grant him credit for his substantial life experience and told him he would have to take the same classes as any other freshman. Realizing that he would be 50 years old by the time he completed college and medical school, Thomas withdrew his application.

PACKED LECTURE HALLS

By the time Vivien Thomas began reconsidering college, Alfred Blalock was no longer thinking much about his now-not-so-underpaid assistant. On August 22, 1947, Blalock, Henry Bahnson, and their wives departed on the luxury ocean liner *Mauretania* for a European tour, during which Blalock and Bahnson would demonstrate the blue baby operation to surgeons in several countries. The tour began in London, where Blalock spent a month at Guy's Hospital as part of an exchange program between British and American surgeons. Blalock and Bahnson operated on 10 children with tetralogy of Fallot during that month, and their success with all 10 patients helped to convince skeptical surgeons that surgical treatment of congenital heart disease was possible.

Partway through that busy month, Blalock and Helen Taussig, who had traveled to England separately, spoke about their groundbreaking operation in the Great Hall of the British Medical Association, which was packed with excited surgeons. Taussig spoke first, followed by Blalock. Russell Brock (later Lord Brock), a well-known British surgeon, recalled the end of Blalock's talk in a 1965 memoir:

> The silence of the audience betokened their rapt attention and appreciation. The hall was quite dark for projection of [Blalock's] slides which had been illustrating patients before and after operation, when suddenly a long searchlight beam traveled the whole length of the hall and unerringly picked out on the platform a Guy's nursing sister, dressed in her attractive blue uniform, sitting on a chair and holding a small cherub-like girl of 2½ years with a halo of blonde curly hair and looking pink and well; she had been operated on at Guy's by Blalock a week earlier. The effect was dramatic and theatrical and the applause of the audience was tumultuous. . . . No audience could fail to have been convinced or satisfied by this summation and no one there could possibly forget it.

Brock was equally impressed by a second speech that Blalock made during the meeting of the International Society of Surgery, held that year in

London at the hall of Britain's premier surgical association, the Royal College of Surgeons. Brock wrote:

> The audience was so large that it only can be described as phenomenal. It literally packed the lecture hall, all adjacent rooms, and the large entrance hall of the College, and overflowed through the main doors to the street. Loudspeakers enabled those outside the lecture hall to hear Blalock speak, but . . . after completing his lecture he acceded to urgent requests and immediately delivered it a second time. . . . The almost delirious acclaim he received dwarfed all the other great lecturers of the earlier days of the week.

Henry Bahnson added in an interview with Mark Ravitch in 1965, "It was said that never before had the hall been half so full and the Professor did it twice."

Blalock's trip through Europe, in fact, turned into what Mark Ravitch's biographical sketch in *The Papers of Alfred Blalock* called "a royal progress." He briefly visited Stockholm, Sweden, to meet with fellow pioneer heart surgeon Clarence Crafoord (1899–1983). He and Bahnson then continued to Paris, where they remained for several weeks and performed surgeries to close an open ductus arteriosus and to treat tetralogy of Fallot. (Helen Taussig had visited Paris several months before to select children for the operations.) The French government made both Blalock and Taussig Chevaliers of the Legion of Honor during this trip. Blalock and Bahnson received so much praise during the tour that (according to Longmire's diary) Blalock told Mary as they boarded the plane that would take them home, "Now we will have to come down to earth again."

HONORS FOR TAUSSIG

Helen Taussig did not share most of Alfred Blalock's European triumphs, but she was receiving new acclaim at Hopkins during the same period. She was finally promoted to the rank of associate professor in the medical school in 1946, and her textbook *Congenital Malformations of the Heart* was published in 1947. This book, based on Taussig's years of diagnostic experience and extensive autopsy examinations of malformed hearts, became the "bible" of pediatric cardiology, the new specialty that she was founding. Taussig would publish a revised edition of the book in 1960.

Like Blalock, Taussig had throngs of eager students who "worshipped her," as Blalock resident Alex Haller put it. Like Blalock, too, she formed life-long relationships with the best of the young men and women who studied under her. Some of them called themselves "the Loyal Knights of Taussig." Just as Alfred Blalock's "boys" went on to teach and pioneer cardiac surgery at hospitals and universities throughout the country, Helen Taussig's "boys"—and "girls"—did the same for pediatric cardiology.

Heart Surgery
Comes of Age

In 1950, Alfred Blalock was due to operate on his 1,000th "blue baby." To celebrate the occasion, Johns Hopkins hired famous Canadian portrait photographer Yousuf Karsh to photograph Blalock at work. Much later, around 1980, Karsh photographed Helen Taussig as well. He produced many photos that are still memorable: Blalock gazing at a photo of one of his blue babies, Blalock with his inevitable cigarette, Taussig tenderly holding one of her young patients, and even a closeup of Taussig's sensitive hands as she examined a child.

The 1,000th operation offered Taussig as well as Blalock a chance to reflect on what the two of them had achieved so far. Having formed a close bond with the blue babies and their families, she had kept track of them and learned how they fared in the years after their surgery. Most, she found, had done well. She made a follow-up report on the first 500 of those children before the first World Congress of Cardiology in Paris in 1950, and the audience gave her a standing ovation.

THUNDER AND LIGHTNING

Unaccompanied by photographers or applauding audiences, Vivien Thomas kept busy in the laboratory. Beginning in 1950, he helped Jerome H. Kay, a postdoctoral fellow in surgical research, investigate ways to restart hearts that had stopped or had gone into *fibrillation*, a state in which the fibers of the

Johns Hopkins invited the famous Canadian portrait photographer Yousuf Karsh to photograph Alfred Blalock in 1950 to commemorate Blalock's 1,000th blue baby operation. This Karsh photo shows Blalock with his inevitable cigarette and a picture of one of the children whose health his surgery had restored. *(© Estate of Yousuf Karsh)*

heart muscle twitch randomly rather than contracting together in their normal, orderly pattern of beats. These conditions can arise during surgery or as the result of illness or accident. If not reversed immediately, they cause death.

William B. Kouwenhoven (1886–1975), an electrical engineer at Johns Hopkins, had studied these heart problems in the 1920s and early 1930s at the request of electric power companies, which were trying to reduce the number of deaths from electrocution among electrical linemen. Kouwenhoven's group had found that shocking the heart with an electric current could both start and stop fibrillation. Kay learned that Kouwenhoven was still at the university; indeed, he was currently the dean of its school of engineering, professor of electrical engineering, and chairman of the electrical engineering department at Hopkins's Homewood campus. Kay contacted the respected engineer and asked him to make a shock device that could be used experimentally on dogs.

Kouwenhoven's machine, Vivien Thomas wrote in his autobiography, was "more or less an assembly of parts on a wooden table," but it did the job. Kay found that after using the device to cause fibrillation, he could squeeze the heart rhythmically by hand, imitating a somewhat slowed form of its regular beat, for anywhere from a few minutes to an hour and then apply a second shock that would make the fibrillation stop. The dogs recovered and showed no signs of brain damage from lack of oxygen, even though their hearts had been unable to work on their own for extended periods.

After Kay demonstrated his results to Blalock, Blalock asked Kay and Kouwenhoven to make an electric *defibrillator* that could be used in the operating room if a patient's heart began fibrillating during surgery. Thomas assembled the defibrillator on the basis of Kouwenhoven's instructions, and the device worked so well that he made several more for other institutions.

Kouwenhoven had become a regular visitor to the old Hunterian building during his work with Kay and Thomas. When he retired from the electrical engineering department in 1954, Blalock offered him a laboratory on the top floor of the building so he could continue his research. There he began a search for a way to stop fibrillation without opening the chest, so that the treatment could be given to people who were not already on the operating table.

Some of Kouwenhoven's experiments involved electric currents carrying as much as 4,000 volts of power. When a capacitor carrying this much current discharged, Thomas wrote, it made a crack like lightning. He and Kouwenhoven had an agreement (made only partly as a joke) that if the lightning was ever followed by thunder—that is, the sound of a human body hitting the floor—Thomas or an assistant was to run upstairs and put the fallen person on one of the laboratory's animal respirators to keep him alive until help could be summoned from the hospital. Fortunately, he and Kouwenhoven never had to test this system.

OPEN-HEART SURGERY

Meanwhile, in operating rooms elsewhere in the country, other surgeons were beginning to extend the trail that Blalock, Taussig, and Thomas had blazed. Until this time, true heart surgery had been all but impossible because the heart was constantly in motion and no one dared to stop it or cut it open. Surgeons knew that if they did so, blood circulation would cease and the patient would die from lack of oxygen within minutes.

Even though there was as yet no way to safely stop the heart, surgeons in the early 1950s found a way to slow it down. In September 1952, John Lewis, a surgeon then at the University of Minnesota, cooled the body of a five-year-old girl to 86° F (30° C) by wrapping her in a blanket through which cold alcohol circulated before operating on her. Lowering body temperature slows down all the body's basic functions and therefore reduces its need for oxygen; it also slows the heartbeat.

Animal experiments had shown that at this temperature, blood flow through the heart could be cut off for as much as 10 minutes without damaging the brain. That precious 10 minutes was time enough for Lewis to sew up a hole between the atria of his little patient's heart. This was the same defect that Vivien Thomas had created in dogs as a treatment for transposition of the aorta and pulmonary artery; like an open ductus arteriosus, it could be helpful in making up for another defect but caused severe health problems when it occurred by itself. Lewis's operation was the first successful *open-heart surgery.*

Lowering body temperature, or *hypothermia,* was a useful technique, but it was also risky. A leak of air into the heart could make the heart muscle begin fibrillating, or the brain could be permanently damaged by lack of oxygen if the surgery (and therefore the circulation stoppage) took longer than expected. A way to stop the heart entirely without stopping the circulation would be better, surgeons realized, but in order to do so, they would need a machine that could take over the work of the heart and lungs while an operation was going on.

A research surgeon named John H. Gibbon, Jr. (1903–73), invented such a device and used it on a human being for the first time in 1953. Gibbon's heart-lung machine was groundbreaking, but it was also expensive, complex, and difficult to use. Surgeons and surgical inventors found many ways to improve the technology of heart-lung machines (or *oxygenators,* as they were professionally called) during the following several years, and with these improvements came equally speedy advances in heart surgery. Among them were some that spelled, if not the end, at least a great decline in the need for the blue baby operation. That operation, lifesaving as it had been, simply eased or made up for the defects that children with tetralogy of Fallot suffered rather than correcting them. With open-heart surgery, actual correction became possible.

THE HEART-LUNG MACHINE

The heart-lung machine was invented because a doctor could not stand to see a patient die. In 1930, while John H. Gibbon, Jr., was still a surgical resident at the University of Pennsylvania Hospital, he assisted in an operation to remove a large blood clot that was blocking a woman's pulmonary artery. This required closing off her major blood vessels temporarily. The brain can survive without oxygen from the blood for just six minutes. The operation took seven minutes, and the woman died.

Spurred by this tragedy, Gibbon and his wife, Mary, began work on a machine that could take over the function of the heart and lungs during surgery. A pump substituted for the heart, sending blood from the body into the machine. Inside the machine, the blood was spread in a thin film on a wire screen in a turning metal cylinder. Oxygen was blown onto this film. The blood, carrying its load of the precious gas, was then pumped back into the body. With the patient's oxygen needs supplied by the machine, the heart potentially could be stopped for hours.

After testing versions of his device on animals for many years, Gibbon used it for the first time on a human patient on May 6, 1953, at Jefferson Medical College in Philadelphia. Like Lewis's hypothermia operation, Gibbon's surgery closed a hole in the wall between the atria. The patient, an 18-year-old college student named Cecelia Bavolek, was on the heart-lung machine for 45 minutes. For 26 minutes of that time, her heart was completely stopped. She not only survived the operation but was still alive and healthy in 2008.

In 1954, within a few months of each other, surgeons H. William Scott at Vanderbilt University and C. Walton Lillehei (1918–99) at the University of Minnesota in Minneapolis carried out the first operations that repaired the defects in patients with tetralogy of Fallot. Scott slowed his patient's heart with hypothermia; Lillehei used a technique he had developed called cross-circulation, in which the child's blood was temporarily pumped through its mother's body to receive oxygen and then returned. Later operations used improved oxygenators instead of either of these riskier, more limited techniques. The blue baby operation continued to be used on children who were

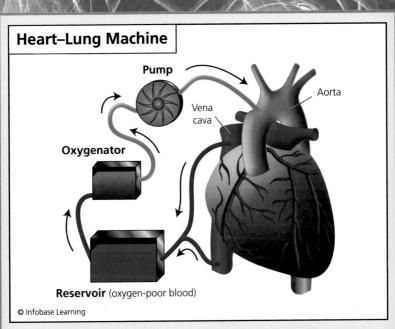

Heart–Lung Machine

Pump

Aorta

Vena cava

Oxygenator

Reservoir (oxygen-poor blood)

© Infobase Learning

A heart-lung machine, or oxygenator, takes over the job of providing oxygen to circulating blood so that the heart can be stopped during surgery. As shown in this diagram, oxygen-depleted blood from the vena cava, the large vein that normally enters the heart's right atrium, is sent through tubing into a reservoir. From there it travels to a part of the device in which the blood is mixed with oxygen. In the first heart-lung machine, invented by John H. Gibbon, Jr., the blood was spread in a thin film on a wire screen in a turning metal cylinder, and oxygen was blown onto this film; later heart-lung machines used a variety of other mechanisms. A pump sends the oxygenated blood back into the aorta so it can circulate through the body.

not strong enough to survive the more extensive open-heart surgery, but the new operation replaced it in most cases.

Alfred Blalock did not learn open-heart surgery techniques. Now in his 50s, he told Vivien Thomas, "Let's face it, Vivien, we're getting older. These young fellows can do a much better job than I can. There's no point in my beating myself out with them around." Nonetheless, he did not want Hopkins to miss out on the new trend. In 1955, therefore, he assigned Henry Bahnson, by then a regular member of the hospital staff, and Frank Spencer, who had just completed his residency, to develop an open-heart surgery program at the hospital. In the first years of the program, Vivien Thomas often cleaned and operated the oxygenator during surgeries, as well as repairing it when it developed mechanical problems.

TRAINING WITH VIVIEN

The new open-heart surgery program was not the only change going on in the venerable Hopkins hospital and medical school. Plans to rebuild parts of the hospital, including its research facilities, were well underway by 1953, and Alfred Blalock played a major part in the project. He visited the research center at the Mayo Clinic in Rochester, Minnesota, in November of that year and was very impressed with their animal care facilities. In December, therefore, he sent a committee, including Vivien Thomas, to study the Mayo arrangements in more detail, with an eye toward designing similar ones at Hopkins. When Thomas expressed doubt that he would be allowed to stay in any of the city's hotels, Blalock arranged for him to board at the house of the clinic's chief surgeon.

The new surgical research laboratory was finally finished in early 1955, and Thomas and his staff moved into it at the end of March. There Thomas continued, not only his research, but his teaching of medical students, who learned surgery by operating on dogs under his watchful eye. Instructors from the medical school demonstrated operations and surgical techniques, but when the teams of students attempted to duplicate the surgeries, "I was always looking over a shoulder, helping to coach them," Thomas wrote.

Over the years, Thomas had become as beloved a teacher as Blalock and Taussig. "We revered him as we did our professor [Blalock]," David Sabiston, a Blalock resident who went on to become chairman of the surgery department at the Duke University medical school in Durham, North Carolina, told *Washingtonian* writer Katie McCabe. "Even if you'd never seen surgery before, you could do it because Vivien made it look so simple," Denton Cooley added.

Thomas trained technicians and other laboratory employees as well as future surgeons. In carrying out this task, he followed the pattern that Alfred Blalock had used with him: He showed them what to do, then expected them to "get it" and work on their own with a minimum of supervision. He sent many of his technicians off to work at other universities with the surgeons he had also trained. For instance, J. Alex Haller told this story in 1971:

> After I finished my internship . . . at Hopkins, I [went to] . . . the National Institutes of Health [a large federal research facility in Bethesda, Maryland] and worked there in the laboratory. I was the only one there, except for the technician, Mr. Alfred Casper. Casper had spent some time observing Vivien . . . at the Hunterian Laboratory. As I worked with him in the first couple of weeks, on one occasion we got into trouble with some massive bleeding, which I was able to handle fairly well. At the conclusion of the operative procedure, Casper said to me, "Dr. Haller, I was very impressed with the way you handled yourself in that situation." Feeling overly proud of myself, I said to Casper, "Well, I was trained by Dr. Blalock." . . .
>
> A few weeks later again we were operating together and we got into trouble for a second time. I did not know what to do. Casper immediately took over, placed the clamps appropriately [to stop the bleeding] and promptly we got out of trouble. I turned to Casper at the end of it and said, "I certainly appreciated everything you did. You knew exactly how to handle your hands very well, too." He looked me in the eye with a little twinkle and said, "I trained with Vivien."

Thomas did not limit his teaching to his own laboratory. As he said wryly in a 1971 interview, he became what he called the "headache man" for labs all over the country. Doctors who had known him at Johns Hopkins and laboratory workers who had heard about him wrote to him about their "headaches," asking his advice on everything from obscure technical problems to setting up and running an entire laboratory. He always helped them as best he could.

HEIGHTS AND DEPTHS

No longer needing to maintain the frenetic stream of operations he had performed in the late 1940s when the blue baby procedure was new and popular,

Alfred Blalock cut back his surgical schedule in the early 1950s. This gave him more time to spend in the research laboratory, his first love. Merril W. Brown, a late Blalock resident, told William Longmire that during this period, "Apparent good health, a truly vintage period of spectacular residents, and a long season of key presidencies and awards resulted in a happy, busy, and mellow Professor."

The second half of the decade, however, brought tragedy for Blalock. His wife's sociable nature, perhaps combined with what William Longmire called her "difficult and exacting" role as a famous surgeon's spouse, had led her to drink excessively, and around 1953 doctors found that she had cirrhosis, or scarring, of the liver—a potentially fatal condition frequently (though not always) caused by alcohol abuse. She died of this illness in December 1958.

Mary's death left Blalock severely depressed, and he in turn began drinking heavily at the end of his workdays. About a year after her passing, however, Blalock married Alice Seney Waters, a widow who had been a neighbor and good friend of Mary's. With Alice's help, the aging surgeon began to recover some of his old spirits.

A group of Blalock's former chief residents had planned a large party to honor him on his 60th birthday, but he had been so depressed and ill that he had asked them to postpone it. By the time of his 61st birthday he was much better, however, so the party took place on April 2, 1960, at the Southern Hotel in Baltimore. William Longmire reported that 500 or 600 people attended, including well-known surgeons from all over the world. Helen Taussig was one of the speakers at the dinner.

One person who was not invited, strangely enough, was Vivien Thomas. Stefan Timmermans, writing in the April 2003 *Social Studies in Science,* states that Blalock himself told the party organizers not to bring Thomas, perhaps because the surgeon knew that the Southern Hotel was still segregated. Some of the residents, as loyal to Thomas as to Blalock, nonetheless smuggled him in, after which, Timmermans writes, "he watched the party from behind the plants." Thomas did not mention this rejection in his autobiography, but it was described in papers in the Johns Hopkins medical archives. According to Timmermans, Thomas was understandably bitter about his treatment on this occasion.

The late 1950s brought high awards to both Alfred Blalock and Helen Taussig. In late 1954, for instance, they shared the Albert Lasker Award, a highly prestigious American science prize. They also won the Gairdner

Award, a famous Canadian prize, in 1959. Taussig was finally promoted to a full professorship in pediatrics in June 1959, by which time, Sherwin Nuland writes, she was "the best-known and most highly regarded woman physician in the world." Blalock, for his part, "was at the height of his acclaim at home and abroad," William Longmire wrote. "The esteem of his colleagues had been demonstrated by his election to the presidency of many of the most prestigious professional and scholarly societies at home and to honorary fellowships in similar organizations abroad." Only Vivien Thomas remained virtually unknown and unhonored outside his laboratory sphere.

Late Honors

Helen Taussig, like Alfred Blalock, kept in touch with most of the doctors she had trained. She held a reunion every two years for her "knights" at her Baltimore home, and she also entertained them individually whenever they happened to be in town for a visit. One such visit started Taussig on a new contribution to medical history.

SEAL LIMBS

One evening in January 1962, Alois Beuren, a German pediatric cardiologist who had once been Taussig's student, was her guest at dinner. During the evening's conversation he mentioned a medical mystery that had recently disturbed German physicians: the occurrence of a terrible but usually rare set of birth defects seemed to be rising, and no one was sure why. Children with this group of defects, called *phocomelia* or "seal limbs," were born without arms and, sometimes, legs. Their flipperlike hands and feet were attached directly to their bodies. Sometimes they had missing ears, partly paralyzed faces, or other problems as well. Only 15 cases of phocomelia had been reported in the medical literature between 1950 and 1958, but 12 children were born with the condition in 1959. The year 1961 had brought 26 such births.

Most of the earlier phocomelia cases were thought to have been inherited, but the new ones were occurring in families where the defect had never

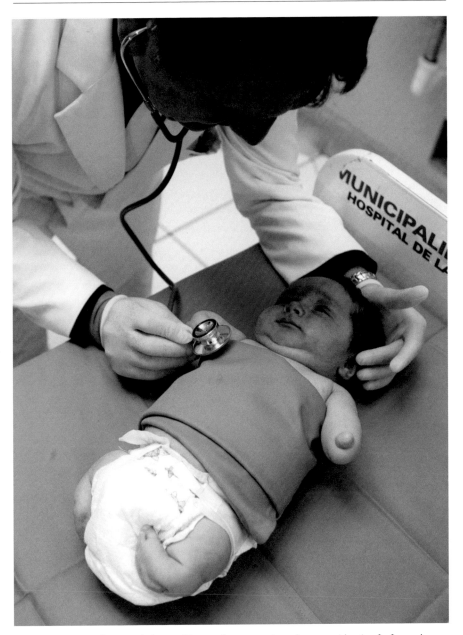

In January 1962, Helen Taussig learned from a former student that an epidemic of a formerly rare set of birth defects called phocomelia, or seal limbs, had broken out in Germany. She helped to spread the word that the defects could be caused by a supposedly harmless medication called thalidomide. Although thalidomide is no longer given to pregnant women, children with phocomelia are still born occasionally. The one shown here was photographed in Lima, Peru, in 2006. *(Pilar Olivares/Reuters/Landov)*

appeared before. Theories about the cause of this mini-epidemic included viruses, secret radiation poisoning by the Russians (this was the time of cold war, when Western countries were extremely concerned about threats from the Soviet Union), and a popular sleeping drug called *thalidomide*. Thalidomide had been considered so harmless that it was prescribed for young children; Taussig later called it "West Germany's babysitter." It was also recommended for pregnant women as a way to control their daily nausea, or morning sickness. People could even buy it without a prescription. Still, the drug had first been sold in 1957, not long before the increase in these births began.

Although Helen Taussig's career had focused on defects involving the heart, she had a lifelong interest in all birth defects, and Beuren's tale of the unlucky seal-limbed children struck her forcefully. Nonetheless, she scolded herself in a later interview for being "a little slow on the uptake" because "I didn't realize until the next morning that I had to go abroad to find out for

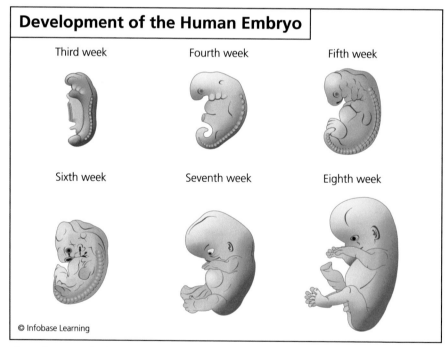

Development of the Human Embryo

Third week

Fourth week

Fifth week

Sixth week

Seventh week

Eighth week

© Infobase Learning

The early stages of a child's development before birth are the most crucial. Development of a human embryo from the third to the eighth week of pregnancy is shown here. Thalidomide was most likely to cause defects if the mother took it between the fourth and sixth weeks, when the embryo's limbs, ears, heart, and digestive system were forming.

myself about this drug and the deformities it [might have] caused." She arranged to take a short leave of absence from Hopkins, lined up several small grants to pay for her trip, and departed two weeks after she had spoken to Beuren. She arrived in Germany on February 1.

Taussig spoke with Widukind Lenz (1919–95), a physician in Hamburg who had investigated possible causes of the seal-limb defects. Lenz had sent a questionnaire to women who gave birth to deformed babies, asking about their exposure during pregnancy to many possible toxins, including X-rays, food additives, and drugs. About one-fifth of the women mentioned taking Contergan, the trade name under which thalidomide was sold in Germany. Lenz then sent a second letter to all the women in his study, asking them specifically if they had used Contergan, and if so at what stage in their pregnancy they had done so. About half the women admitted that they had taken the pills; most said they had neglected to list the drug on the first questionnaire because they thought it too harmless and unimportant to be worth mentioning. Many of the women had swallowed the drug between the 20th and 40th days of pregnancy, Lenz found; even one pill taken during that period was sometimes enough to produce a deformed child.

After Lenz announced his results in November 1961, the Swiss company that made Contergan withdrew it from the German market. By this time, physicians in several other countries where thalidomide was sold were making discoveries similar to Lenz's.

Helen Taussig knew that unborn children's arms and legs formed during the period of pregnancy that Lenz had found to be critical, so his ideas made sense to her. By the end of her European trip, which included a visit to Britain (where thalidomide was also sold and phocomelia births had occurred), she was all but certain that thalidomide caused these bizarre and tragic birth defects.

PREVENTING A DISASTER

Thalidomide was not yet sold in the United States. The William S. Merrell Company, a pharmaceutical firm, had applied to the federal Food and Drug Administration (FDA) in September 1960 for permission to sell it, but the company's application lay ungranted on the desk of a suspicious FDA staff physician named Frances Kelsey (1914–   ). "The claims were just too glowing—too good to be true," Kelsey wrote later. In particular, she was concerned because she had read reports that the drug had sometimes produced tingling, numbness, and other signs of nerve damage in people who took it.

Frances O. Kelsey (1914–   ), a physician working for the U.S. Food and Drug Administration, was suspicious of thalidomide and refused to allow it to be sold unless its safety could be demonstrated. Helen Taussig confirmed Kelsey's doubts. The actions of these two women prevented an epidemic of phocomelia birth defects in the United States and led to stricter laws concerning the testing and distribution of new drugs. Kelsey is shown here in 1963, shortly after the thalidomide crisis. *(Photograph by Art Rickerby/Time Life Pictures/Getty Images)*

She therefore refused to grant permission for its sale unless the Merrell Company provided convincing evidence that it was safe.

Even though the FDA had not approved thalidomide, Helen Taussig learned that physicians and their patients could obtain the drug in several ways. It was sold legally in countries as close as Canada, and people sometimes bought it during visits to those countries. At the time, drug companies also could give unapproved medications like thalidomide to physicians if they labeled the compounds as "new" or "investigative" drugs. Doctors sometimes prescribed the medications without mentioning their status to patients. Records later showed that about 1,200 physicians in the United

States had prescribed thalidomide, and 16,000 people, including 200 pregnant women, had taken it.

Because thalidomide was available, even if not widely so, Taussig knew she had to warn physicians about its danger to pregnant women and their unborn children as quickly as possible. As soon as she returned from her European trip, she began making speeches about the drug, first to an audience at Johns Hopkins and then in a special added session during the annual meeting of the American College of Physicians on April 11, 1962. She also wrote articles or editorials about thalidomide for influential scientific publications including *Scientific American, The Journal of the American Medical Association,* and *Science.*

In addition, Taussig met with Frances Kelsey and told Kelsey everything she had learned in Europe. By this time, word about thalidomide's role in the seal-limb disaster was spreading, and Merrell had withdrawn its application. Because thousands of doses of thalidomide still lay in doctors' offices and home medicine cabinets, however, the FDA, under Kelsey's direction, launched a "pill-by-pill search" for physicians and hospitals who had received the drug. Newspapers warned all women of childbearing age who had thalidomide in their homes to throw it away.

A total of about 10,000 seal-limb babies were born in Africa and Europe, but Taussig and Kelsey's prompt actions ensured that only 17 such children appeared in the United States. The tragic thalidomide story, furthermore, highlighted the fact that even medications harmless to most people could cause severe birth defects if taken by pregnant women—something that even most physicians did not realize at the time. The case also pointed out the dangers of allowing drugs not yet approved by the FDA to be distributed to doctors. President John F. Kennedy (1917–63) and some members of Congress had already been urging that drug-approval laws be tightened, and the thalidomide case provided the additional evidence they needed to obtain passage of the new laws. The revised laws, which required testing drugs for safety during pregnancy and forbade distributing new drugs before FDA approval had been obtained, went into effect in February 1963.

A LIFESAVING DEVICE

Alfred Blalock frequently visited Vivien Thomas in the new surgical laboratory to discuss research ideas, but Thomas wrote in his autobiography that none of the projects Blalock proposed in the early 1960s bore much fruit. Thomas admitted that this slower pace was something of a relief to him. As the

HORMONE DISRUPTORS

Helen Taussig and Frances Kelsey are not the only women scientists who have warned the public that seemingly harmless substances may present unusual dangers to the unborn. Beginning around 1990, Theodora (Theo) Colborn (1927–   ), a New Jersey-born environmental scientist, and others have claimed that a variety of pollutants and industrial chemicals, including some in pesticides and commonly used plastics, can damage the bodies of humans and animals during development by affecting the action of *hormones*. Hormones are natural substances that send long-distance messages from one group of cells to another. They control a variety of body processes, including reproduction and the development of young animals before birth.

Chemicals that alter the behavior of hormones in unnatural ways are called *endocrine disruptors*. (The endocrine system consists of hormones and the small organs called glands that make them.) Some endocrine disruptors change the effects of hormones by mimicking the hormones and making the body act as if the hormones were present when they actually are not. Others block the action of existing hormones. Colborn and other researchers have tied endocrine disruptors to reproduction problems and deformed or sickly offspring in wildlife. They claim that even tiny amounts of these compounds entering a human baby's body before or shortly after birth can damage its developing brain, immune system, and reproductive system, producing loss of intelligence, abnormal behavior, physical deformities, and lifelong harm to health. Colborn (with coauthors Dianne Dumanoski and John Peter Meyers) described these dangers in a 1996 book called *Our Stolen Future*.

Not all scientists think that low doses of endocrine disruptors are as dangerous as Colborn and her supporters say they are. However, the federal Environmental Protection Agency (EPA) has taken the threat of these chemicals seriously enough to plan a massive program to screen some 87,000 substances for their effects on hormones. The Endocrine Disruptor Screening Program (EDSP) began screening chemicals in October 2009.

acting, even if unofficial, head of the laboratory, he found so much of his time taken up with administrative chores and "headache man" consultations with researchers and their assistants that he had little time left for his own work.

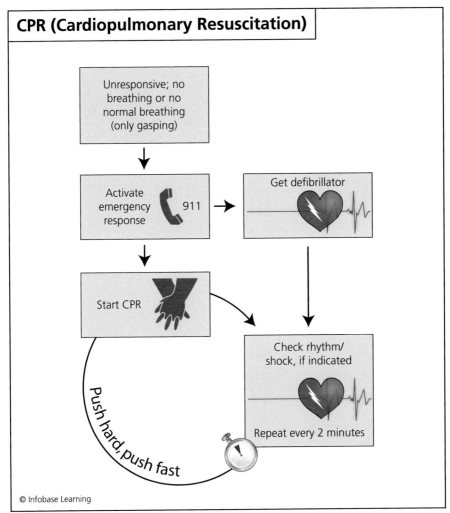

CPR (Cardiopulmonary Resuscitation)

Unresponsive; no breathing or no normal breathing (only gasping)

Activate emergency response — 911

Get defibrillator

Start CPR

Check rhythm/ shock, if indicated

Repeat every 2 minutes

Push hard, push fast

© Infobase Learning

Research at Johns Hopkins, in some of which Vivien Thomas took part, led to development of the commonly used rescue technique called cardiopulmonary resuscitation, or CPR. As this diagram shows, current American Heart Association guidelines (revised in 2010) stress hard, fast chest compressions—pressing down at least two inches (five cm) for an adult, at least 100 times a minute—and use of a defibrillator if it is available. Chest compressions massage the heart and keep it beating rhythmically.

Important research still took place in the surgical laboratory, however. The most exciting results came from William Kouwenhoven's continuing project on restarting stopped or fibrillating hearts. Massaging or shocking the heart directly was practical when a patient already lay, with chest opened, on an operating table, but it was of little use to a person on the street who suffered, say, an accident or a sudden heart attack. Kouwenhoven and his coworkers therefore looked for ways to apply these types of treatments when the chest was closed. They first developed an electrical defibrillator, which they began using on human patients at Johns Hopkins in March 1957. This machine was too cumbersome to be portable, but later, smaller models became (and still are) standard equipment in ambulances and hospital emergency rooms.

G. Guy Knickerbocker, a colleague of Kouwenhoven's, meanwhile noticed that in the group's experimental dogs, sometimes simply pressing the heavy electrodes of the defibrillator firmly onto an animal's chest was enough to raise the dog's blood pressure, a sign of returning circulation. Knickerbocker began to investigate the idea that rhythmic pressure on the closed chest could act as the equivalent of cardiac massage. He developed a technique for repeated presses on the chest, which was combined with mouth-to-mouth breathing (developed by two other researchers, James O. Elam [1918–95] and Peter Safar [1924–2003] of Hopkins's anesthesiology staff) to form the now-common emergency revival technique of *cardiopulmonary resuscitation,* or *CPR.* Henry Bahnson first used this technique on a two-year-old child in February 1958, and Kouwenhoven and others began teaching it to Baltimore ambulance crews in 1959.

Kouwenhoven's team reported on their research at a meeting of the American Surgical Association in March 1961. In the discussion that followed the group's paper, Blalock said, "There are two things of great interest to me in this project. One is that most important discoveries are simple in concept and design, and the [other] . . . is that an occasional person past three score and ten [70 years of age] makes an important discovery." Old age and, in particular, retirement were very much on Blalock's mind because he was facing his own, which was scheduled for 1964.

ALL-TOO-SHORT RETIREMENT

In some ways, Alfred Blalock's career at Johns Hopkins ended, as it had begun, in bitterness. Blalock felt that he should have been allowed to choose his successor as chief of surgery, a position he wanted one of his mentees to have. In January 1964, however, the Johns Hopkins selection committee picked a young surgeon named George Zuidema (1928–), who had gone to medical school at Hopkins but took his surgical training at Massachusetts

General Hospital in Boston. Just as the Hopkins surgical staff had said regarding Blalock himself in 1941, Blalock claimed that Zuidema was not sufficiently mature or experienced for this post. William Longmire wrote that Blalock carried his campaign against the younger man "well beyond the limits of academic propriety," but the selection committee refused to change their minds. This clash between Blalock and the Hopkins administrators produced considerable anger on both sides.

Even this bad feeling could make little dent in the great admiration with which almost everyone regarded Blalock, however. When the Hopkins hospital celebrated its 75th anniversary on May 14, 1964, Blalock was chosen to give the main address at the festivity's evening banquet. He had to speak sitting down because unexplained pain in his back, which began in early 1963, had become so severe that he could not stand for any length of time. He had surgery for this back problem a few days before the ceremony, but it brought little relief.

During this same celebration, Walter Perkins, chairman of the Johns Hopkins Hospital's board of trustees, announced a further honor: The hospital's clinical sciences building, in whose creation Blalock had played such an important part, would hereafter be known as the Alfred Blalock Clinical Sciences Building. A portrait of Blalock, painted by Isabel Hunner Parsons in 1945, would hang in the building's lobby. William Longmire wrote in his diary: "With this announcement, bedlam broke loose. Everyone stood to applaud; there were shouts of Hooray! from all over the room . . . Al just shook his head in disbelief."

Blalock retired on July 1, 1964. Several universities at which his protégés held important posts had offered him part-time positions, but he said he did not want to leave Hopkins. The sad truth was that he was too sick to do so. Further operations had somewhat relieved his back pain, but it never entirely went away, and by mid-1964 it was obvious that the surgeon was seriously ill. No one knew the exact cause, but they began to suspect cancer.

Blalock was admitted to Johns Hopkins Hospital, weak and confused, during the first week of August and died there on September 15, 1964. An autopsy revealed that a cancerous tumor had developed around the stump of the ureter (the tube that carries urine from the kidney to the bladder) that remained after his left kidney had been removed during his 20s. The cancer spread to his liver and other organs, causing his back pain and, ultimately, his death.

In May 1964, shortly before Alfred Blalock's retirement, Johns Hopkins's clinical sciences building was given his name. This portrait of Blalock, painted by Isabella Hunner Parsons in 1945, was hung in the building's lobby. *(Alan Mason Chesney Medical Archives of the Johns Hopkins Medical Institutions, photograph by Aaron Levin)*

STAYING ON

Vivien Thomas, 10 years younger than Alfred Blalock and in excellent health, had no plans to retire when Blalock did. As Blalock's departure day neared, therefore, Thomas had to make decisions about his own future career. Knowing that Blalock was thinking about taking a part-time post at another university, Thomas told the surgeon not to include him when making any such plans. Thomas wrote in his autobiography that he took this stand because he did not want to limit Blalock's choices to places that would be willing to make room for an African American. Partly too, as always, he wanted to maintain his independence.

Thomas was well aware that the decision about whether he would remain at Hopkins did not rest entirely with him. He would need the approval of George Zuidema, the new chief of surgery, in order to continue at the surgical laboratory. Zuidema had probably heard that Blalock had bitterly opposed his appointment, and Thomas surely must have wondered whether Zuidema would be willing to keep someone so closely associated with Blalock. The new chief might well, as Barney Brooks had done when Blalock prepared to leave Vanderbilt, tell Thomas that there would be "no place" for him once Blalock was gone.

Thomas's anxiety increased as several months passed after Zuidema's appointment without any word about whether Thomas would be invited to stay. With his usual practicality, therefore, Thomas set about learning what options he had outside of Hopkins. In May 1964, he visited Indiana University at Indianapolis, where Harris B. Shumacker, one of Blalock's residents who had spent quite a bit of time in Thomas's laboratory, was professor of surgery. He also called on H. William Scott, another former Hopkins resident, who was then chairman of the department of surgery at Thomas's old home, Vanderbilt University. Both men told him that he would be welcome at their universities if he wished to move there.

When Thomas walked into his office on the day he returned from this trip, he heard his phone ringing: Zuidema wanted to see him at 10 o'clock. During their meeting, he told Zuidema about his recent travels and the offers he had received. "I hope you enjoyed your trip, but you can just forget the rest, because we want you to remain here," Zuidema told him. He assured Thomas that Thomas could go on unofficially running the laboratory, answering only to Zuidema himself, just as he had done with Blalock.

Thomas therefore continued as before. Now involved mostly in supervisory and administrative work, he did not have a chance to work on another important research project until 1970. At that time he headed one of two surgical teams carrying out experimental lung transplants in baboons.

HANGING TOGETHER

Vivien Thomas spent little time thinking about the honors that Alfred Blalock and Helen Taussig had received for their contributions to medicine, sure that no equivalent would ever come to him. Fortunately, he was wrong. A group of Blalock's former chief residents, who called themselves the Old Hands Club, remembered how much they had learned, not only from their inspiring and revered "Professor," but from his unsung assistant as well. At a meeting in February 1969, the club voted to commission a portrait of Thomas to be painted and hung in the Hopkins hospital.

The portrait, painted by Bob Gee, was unveiled at a ceremony honoring Thomas on February 27, 1971. Thomas wrote that he felt strange being in the limelight, but it was "the most emotional and gratifying experience of my life." He expected that the portrait would be hung near the elevator on the floor where his laboratory was. In fact, however, Russell Nelson (1913–2001), the hospital's president, announced in his presentation speech that Thomas's portrait would be placed next to Blalock's in the clinical sciences building's main lobby. "We think you 'hung' together [in life] and you had better continue to hang together," Nelson said.

The Civil Rights movement of the 1960s had opened up new opportunities for African Americans, so Thomas had many chances in the 1970s and early 1980s to help others of his race. Some he trained for laboratory work. For example, he spotted Raymond Lee operating an elevator at Hopkins and asked him if he wanted to learn to be a technician. Lee later became the first person without an M.D. degree to serve on Hopkins's cardiac surgery service; Alex Haller called him "another Vivien." Another of Thomas's black trainees was a woman, Jean Queen, who had worked in the hospital's laundry room before Thomas offered her a laboratory job. She eventually became the laboratory manager.

Thomas helped other African Americans achieve goals that he had not been able to reach himself. Perhaps the best known of these was Levi Watkins, Jr. (1945–   ), who, Katie McCabe wrote in her *Washingtonian* article, became "everything Vivien Thomas might have been had he been born 40 years later." Watkins graduated with honors from Tennessee State, the college that Thomas had planned to attend before the Great Depression derailed his dreams. Watkins then followed Thomas's path to Vanderbilt University's medical school, but instead of being a technician in its laboratory he attended the school itself, becoming its first African-American graduate. Finally, he moved on to Johns Hopkins, where he became the medical school's first African-American chief resident in cardiac surgery.

This portrait of Vivien Thomas, painted by Bob Gee, was unveiled at a ceremony honoring Thomas on February 27, 1971. The portrait was hung next to Alfred Blalock's in the lobby of the Hopkins clinical sciences building. *(Alan Mason Chesney Medical Archives of the Johns Hopkins Medical Institutions, photograph by Aaron Levin)*

Watkins first met Thomas in the hospital cafeteria a few weeks after he came to Hopkins as an intern in 1971, when he recognized Thomas as "the man in the picture" in the lobby. "That marked the beginning of a fourteen-year friendship," Watkins wrote in a memorial chapter about Thomas in *A Century of Black Surgeons*. Not surprisingly, the two formed a deep bond. "I

Levi Watkins, Jr. (1945–   ), was one of a number of African Americans whose careers Vivien Thomas mentored. Watkins was the first African-American graduate of Vanderbilt University and the first African-American chief resident in cardiac surgery at Johns Hopkins. He went on to become a professor of surgery at Hopkins. Watkins and Thomas helped to invent the automatic implantable defibrillator, and Watkins placed the first such device in a human patient in 1980. This photograph of Watkins was taken during his years at Vanderbilt. (*Vanderbilt University*)

knew that he had been where I had been, and I had been where he could not go," Watkins said to Katie McCabe.

Nonetheless, being born 40 years apart created major differences in attitude between the two men, McCabe pointed out. A child of the Civil Rights movement, Watkins was "out front and vocal about minority participation" in all spheres of life. Thomas, however, had lived in an era in which such an approach would have been fruitless, if not actually dangerous. Used to thinking of survival first, Thomas worried about Watkins "being too political and antagonizing the people I had to work with," Watkins recalled. At the same time, he was very proud of Watkins, especially when Watkins joined the medical school admissions committee and, within four years, minority enrollment in the school quadrupled.

In the late 1970s, Watkins and Thomas had a chance to work on a research project together—Watkins's first as a Hopkins faculty member (he eventually became a full professor of surgery there), and Thomas's last. They helped to develop the automatic implantable defibrillator, a descendant of the machines that Kouwenhoven, with Thomas's help, had invented amid artificial thunder and lightning on the top floor of the old Hunterian building. The device could be placed inside a patient's body to automatically shock a weak heart back to normal rhythm each time it began to fibrillate. Watkins implanted the first one into a human patient in 1980, just a few months after Thomas's retirement.

RECOGNITION AT LAST

The portrait and its presentation ceremony were not the only honor that came to Vivien Thomas in his later years. In late March 1976, he received a letter from George H. Callcott, the vice chancellor of the University of Maryland at College Park, saying that the administration, faculty, and students of that university had recommended him for an honorary doctorate. Callcott told him that the proposal had yet to be approved by the university's board of regents, but he expected their vote to be a mere formality.

Unfortunately, Callcott was wrong. On April 12, he wrote to Thomas with "embarrassment and sadness" that the regents had rejected the proposal. The reason they gave was that the College Park campus had no medical school, so it should not grant an honor to a person "distinguished in medicine." Whether Thomas's race played any role in their decision is unknown, but that possibility is bound to have crossed the disappointed man's mind.

Thomas did not remain disappointed for long, however. Just a few days after the arrival of Callcott's letter, he received another from Johns Hopkins president Steven Muller saying that the Hopkins board of trustees had voted to award him an honorary degree of their own. Ironically, for reasons that remain unclear, the degree would be a doctorate of laws, a field Thomas had never studied, rather than of medicine. Thomas received his degree as part of the yearly commencement ceremony on May 21, 1976, along with a huge ovation.

Now that Thomas finally had a doctor's degree, he asked for and received two more belated tokens of recognition from the university he had served for so long. First, in January 1977, he was given the position of instructor in surgery. Later that year, he was made the official head of the laboratory that he had run in all but name for so many years. Thomas kept these titles until his retirement on July 1, 1979.

Mark Ravitch, a great admirer of Thomas as well as Blalock, persuaded Thomas to write an autobiography. Thomas began working on the book just after his retirement and completed it in 1985. Unfortunately, he did not live to see it published; Thomas died of pancreatic cancer on November 25, 1985, just days before the first copies appeared.

The story of Vivien Thomas's role in the famous blue baby operation and the development of heart surgery began to spread outside the Hopkins community in 1989, when reporter Katie McCabe wrote an article about him for *Washingtonian* magazine. This article received the National Magazine Award. In 2003, the relationship between Blalock and Thomas was the subject of "Partners of the Heart," a documentary in the Public Broadcasting System's *American Experience* series. This documentary won the Organization of American Historians' Erik Barnouw Award for Best Historical Documentary in 2004. The Blalock-Thomas story was also made into a docudrama called *Something the Lord Made,* staring Alan Rickman as Blalock and former hip-hop singer Mos Def as Thomas. This program, broadcast on Home Box Office (HBO) in 2004, earned an Emmy and a Peabody Award.

A LONG LIFE

Being about the same age as Alfred Blalock, Helen Taussig retired at about the same time, in July 1963. Unlike Blalock, however, Taussig was in excellent health, so she simply went on working at Hopkins part time. Almost one-third of her 129 published papers appeared after her supposed retirement.

Honors continued to come to Taussig as she grew older. The greatest was the Medal of Freedom, the highest award that the U.S. government can give a civilian. President Lyndon Johnson (1908–73) presented this medal to her in 1964. In 1965, she was elected president of the American Heart Association, the first woman ever to hold this high post. The American College of Physicians named her a "master," the highest level of its membership, in 1972, another honor she was the first woman to receive. She was one of the first group of women honored by the Women's Hall of Fame when it opened in 1973, and Hopkins named its new children's cardiac clinic after her in 1974. In May 1976, on Taussig's 78th birthday, her "loyal knights" sponsored an international symposium on pediatric cardiology in her honor. She won the Kober Medal of the Association of American Physicians in May 1986.

One of Taussig's chief projects in later life was an ongoing follow-up of the former "blue babies" who had been restored to health by the Blalock-Taussig operation. In "The Development of the Blalock-Taussig Operation and Its Results Twenty Years Later," a paper Taussig read to the American

Helen Taussig, shown here in a famous photograph taken by Yousuf Karsh around 1980, cared deeply about her tiny patients and formed lifelong relationships with many former "blue babies" and their families. As a result, she was able to track most of these children well into adulthood. She showed that many became well educated, married and started families, and had productive careers, answering the doubts of some who feared that the children's early lack of oxygen had damaged their brains. (© *Estate of Yousuf Karsh*)

Philosophical Society on April 24, 1975, she reported that most of the children with tetralogy of Fallot whom Blalock and other Hopkins surgeons had operated on between 1945 and 1951—685 out of 779 patients—had survived

Helen Taussig, shown here in a portrait displayed at Johns Hopkins, was the last survivor of the three unlikely partners who had revolutionized heart surgery. She died in 1986. *(Alan Mason Chesney Medical Archives of the Johns Hopkins Medical Institutions)*

for at least six years after the surgery, a mortality rate of less than 12 percent. At the 20-year mark, 376 patients were alive and available for follow-up.

Some doubters had feared that, even if the children survived, their brains would prove to have been damaged by their years of living with insufficient oxygen, but Taussig was happy to report that this was not the case. She wrote that 35 percent of the survivors had graduated from college, and 69 percent had "substantial" incomes. About half had married, furthermore, and 161 had one or more children.

On February 11, 1986, Samuel Sanders, a former "blue baby" who had grown up to become a respected concert pianist, performed a recital at the Peabody Museum, part of Johns Hopkins, and dedicated it to Helen Taussig, who was present in the audience. "She was radiantly full of life," Anne Garside, director of public information at the Peabody Institute, told Joyce Baldwin.

Unfortunately, this concert and the ceremony during which Taussig's winning of the Kober Medal was announced were the last times that most of her friends would see her. On May 20, 1986, three days before her 88th birthday, Taussig was killed instantly when another car struck hers. The death of the last of these three oddly matched pioneers—the surgeon, the expert in children's hearts, and the skilled technician—marked the end of the era that had seen the body's last "forbidden" organ, the heart, finally opened to the surgeon's healing touch.

Conclusion

Heart-lung machines were just the beginning of the advances that created the heart surgery of today. Since the 1950s, surgeons have learned how to replace parts of the heart and major blood vessels with both natural and artificial materials. They have even been able to transplant whole hearts.

Some operations replace abnormal blood vessels with healthy vessels taken from elsewhere in the patient's own body. Robert Gross treated coarctation of the aorta in this way as early as the late 1940s, for instance. When he could, Gross simply snipped out the narrowed part of the aorta and rejoined the ends of the cut vessel. Some patients, however, had a narrow section too long to allow such rejoining. In those cases, Gross grafted in a segment of the abdominal artery to replace the missing piece.

One of today's most common heart surgeries is also usually done with a patient's own vessels. It uses these vessels to bypass *coronary arteries*—the vital arteries that nourish the heart itself—that have become blocked with fatty deposits, resulting in chronic chest pain and potentially fatal heart attacks. Sometimes as many as four arteries are bypassed in a single operation. Coronary bypass surgery began in the late 1960s.

Instead of relying on the patient as a source, some heart and blood vessel surgery uses parts from deceased donors who have left permission for their bodies to be used in this way. Some heart valves, which control the flow of blood in that organ, can also be replaced with valves taken from pigs or cattle when the animals are slaughtered for meat. The first pig valve was used in human surgery in 1965.

The most spectacular replacement of all, of course, is the heart itself. The South African surgeon Christiaan Barnard (1922–2001) made the first successful heart transplant on December 3, 1967. The donor was a young woman killed in a car accident. The heart's recipient, Louis Washkansky, died from an infection only 18 days after the surgery, but a second Barnard transplant patient, Philip Blaiberg, survived for almost two years after receiving a new heart in January 1968. Survival for much longer periods became possible after 1980, when Stanford University surgeon Norman Shumway (1923–2006) and others began giving patients *cyclosporine,* a new drug that kept the immune system from attacking the donor heart.

Unfortunately, the number of people who need new hearts is far greater than the number of hearts available for transplant. Researchers therefore began investigating the possibility of building artificial hearts in the late

Heart transplant operations such as the one shown here are just one of the many forms of cardiac surgery that grew out of the pioneering work of Alfred Blalock, Helen Taussig, and Vivien Thomas. *(SHOUT/Alamy)*

1970s. (Artificial heart valves were used much earlier, beginning in the early 1960s.) The University of Utah surgeon William DeVries transplanted the first artificial heart, the Jarvik 7 (named after its inventor, Robert Jarvik), into a patient in December 1982. DeVries's patient, Barney Clark, survived for 112 days, but the need to stay attached to the bulky machine that kept the heart pumping confined him to the hospital. A totally implantable artificial heart kept another patient alive for about the same length of time in 2001. Artificial hearts so far have not been successful enough to come into common use, but small devices that do part of the heart's work are often implanted into patients who are waiting for a heart transplant to become available.

Some operations treat children born with heart defects such as tetralogy of Fallot—Helen Taussig's "little crossword puzzles." Such defects can be revealed by new imaging techniques, sometimes while babies are still in the womb, and usually are repaired surgically in infancy. An article in the July 16, 2008, *Journal of the American Medical Association* reports that in most children born with tetralogy of Fallot today, surgery can repair the defects within three months of birth, with a death rate of only 3 percent. In children whose defects are too complex to repair completely, surgeons sometimes employ a modified form of the blue baby operation, using a shunt vessel made of plastic.

All these forms of heart surgery go far beyond the relatively simple blue baby operation. They use technology that Alfred Blalock, Helen Taussig, and Vivien Thomas could not have imagined when they developed that operation in 1944. The blue baby surgery, however, opened the door to these later advances by proving to surgeons everywhere that operations on the heart and great blood vessels were possible. Blalock, Thomas, and Taussig, furthermore, trained many of the surgeons who first performed these groundbreaking operations. For these reasons, all of today's heart surgery, from coronary bypasses to heart transplants, can be said to be the legacy of these three pioneers.

At Johns Hopkins, Blalock, Taussig, and Thomas have left other legacies as well. Alfred Blalock's name still graces one of the campus's research buildings, and the medical school's division of pediatric cardiology is named after Helen Taussig. One of Hopkins's four advisory colleges for medical students bears Vivien Thomas's name, and a fund has been established, also in Thomas's name, to increase diversity at Hopkins and help members of underrepresented groups gain a medical education. The Web page for the Vivien Thomas Fund points out that by 2004, more than 11 percent of Hopkins's medical students were African American, as were 60 members of its full-time faculty, including star surgeon Levi Watkins. Perhaps this is the tribute that would have pleased Vivien Thomas most of all.

Chronology

May 24, 1898
Helen Brooke Taussig born in Cambridge, Massachusetts

April 5, 1899
Alfred Blalock born in Culloden, Georgia

August 29, 1910
Vivien Theodore Thomas born in Lake Providence, Louisiana

1918
Blalock graduates from University of Georgia, enters Johns Hopkins Medical School

1921
Taussig graduates from University of California, Berkeley

1922
Blalock earns M.D. degree

1924
Taussig enters Johns Hopkins Medical School

July 1, 1925
Blalock becomes chief resident in surgery at hospital of Vanderbilt University (Nashville, Tennessee)

1926
Blalock and Tinsley Harrison do research on cardiac output; Blalock begins research on shock

1927
Blalock develops tuberculosis and takes treatment at Trudeau Sanatorium; Taussig earns M.D. degree

September 1928
Blalock returns to Vanderbilt; is promoted to assistant professor; resumes research on shock

October 1929
Stock market crashes, beginning Great Depression; Thomas loses construction job and defers college plans

1930
Blalock becomes associate professor at Vanderbilt; Taussig loses most of her hearing; she is chosen to head new children's heart clinic at Johns Hopkins Hospital

February 10, 1930
Blalock and Thomas meet; Blalock hires Thomas as laboratory assistant

June 1930
Blalock's most important paper on shock is published

October 25, 1930
Blalock marries Mary O'Brien

November 1930
Thomas loses savings in bank crash, is forced to abandon hope of going to medical school

early 1930s
Blalock and Thomas investigate the chemistry and treatment of shock; Taussig begins to learn about birth defects that affect the heart

December 22, 1933
Thomas marries Clara Flanders

1937
Blalock rejects job offer from Henry Ford Hospital because hospital will not also hire Thomas; is promoted to full professor at Vanderbilt

1938
Blalock, Thomas, and Sanford Levy join subclavian artery to pulmonary artery in dogs in unsuccessful attempt to create high blood pressure in the lung; Taussig visits Maude Abbott to learn more about congenital heart defects

August 26, 1938
Robert Gross performs first operation to close a patent (open) ductus arteriosus

1940
Taussig suggests to Gross that he create an artificial ductus in children with tetralogy of Fallot, but he rejects her idea; Blalock's book *Principles of Surgical Care: Shock and Other Problems* is published

July 1, 1941
Blalock becomes chief of surgery at Johns Hopkins Hospital and professor of surgery at Hopkins medical school; Thomas begins work in hospital's surgical research laboratory

late 1941
Blalock and Thomas begin research on crush syndrome

December 7, 1941
United States declares war on Japan, thus entering World War II, after Japanese bomb U.S. military base at Pearl Harbor, Hawaii

1942
Blalock and Taussig meet in the fall; Taussig suggests possibility of making an open ductus to Blalock

1943
Blalock and Thomas develop operation to treat coarctation of the aorta

1944
Taussig, Blalock, and Thomas develop the blue baby operation (Blalock-Taussig shunt), and Thomas tests it on dogs

November 29, 1944
Blalock performs first blue baby operation on Eileen Saxon

February 1945
Blalock performs successful blue baby operations on two more children

May 19, 1945
Blalock and Taussig's article describing first three blue baby operations is published in *Journal of the American Medical Association*

June 1945
Blue baby operation makes newspaper headlines; Blalock elected to National Academy of Sciences

1945
World War II ends

December 1945
Columbia University attempts to hire Blalock away, but Blalock decides not to go

1946
Thomas develops operation to treat transposition of the great vessels; Taussig promoted to associate professor

December 1946
Blalock appoints C. Rollins Hanlon to direct surgical laboratory; Thomas's salary is doubled after he threatens to quit

1947
Blalock travels to Europe to speak about and demonstrate blue baby operation; Taussig's book *Congenital Malformations of the Heart* is published

1950
Blalock performs 1,000th blue baby operation; Taussig gives follow-up report on first 500 blue babies; Thomas works with Jerome Kay and William Kouwenhoven on ways to treat heart fibrillation

1952
John Lewis performs first successful open-heart surgery, using hypothermia

May 6, 1953
John H. Gibbon, Jr., performs first successful human operation with his heart-lung machine

1954
First operations to correct tetralogy of Fallot performed; Blalock and Taussig share Albert Lasker Award

1955
Blalock assigns two younger surgeons to start open-heart surgery program at Hopkins; new research laboratories open

1957
Thalidomide, a sleep-inducing drug, begins to be sold in Europe and Africa

March 1957
Kouwenhoven's closed-chest electrical defibrillator is used on first human patient

February 1958
Cardiopulmonary resuscitation (CPR) technique used on humans for the first time

December 1958
Mary Blalock dies of cirrhosis of the liver

1959
Blalock and Taussig share Gairdner Prize; Taussig promoted to full professor; number of European children born with phocomelia (seal limbs) suddenly increases

November 1959
Blalock marries Alice Waters

November 1961
Widukind Lenz reports link between thalidomide and phocomelia in Germany; drug's manufacturer withdraws it from the market

January 1962
Taussig hears about epidemic of phocomelia in Germany

February 1962
Taussig travels to Germany and Britain to investigate possible link between phocomelia and thalidomide

April 11, 1962
Taussig speaks to American College of Physicians about thalidomide's danger to pregnant women and unborn children

February 1963
Tighter drug approval laws, passed partly because of the thalidomide scare, go into effect

July 1963
Taussig retires; continues to work part time

May 14, 1964
Blalock gives main speech at Hopkins hospital's 75th anniversary celebration; clinical sciences building is named after him

1964
Taussig receives Medal of Freedom

July 1, 1964
Blalock retires

September 15, 1964
Blalock dies of cancer

1965
Taussig becomes first woman president of American Heart Association

December 3, 1967
Christiaan Barnard performs first heart transplant

February 27, 1971
Portrait of Thomas unveiled in ceremony to honor Thomas and is hung next to Blalock's in lobby of clinical sciences building

1974
New children's heart clinic at Hopkins named after Taussig

1975
Taussig reports on survival and health of former blue babies 20 years after their operations

1976
International symposium on pediatric cardiology held in Taussig's honor

May 21, 1976
Thomas receives honorary doctorate of laws from Johns Hopkins

1977
Thomas made instructor of surgery; named as official head of surgical research laboratory

late 1970s
Thomas and Levi Watkins, Jr., develop implantable automatic defibrillator

July 1, 1979
Thomas retires

1980
Norman Shumway and others introduce cyclosporine, a drug that keeps the immune system from attacking donor hearts or other organs

December 1982
First successful implantation of an artificial heart (the Jarvik 7)

November 25, 1985
Thomas dies of cancer; his autobiography is published a few days later

1986
Taussig wins Kober Medal of the Association of American Physicians

May 26, 1986
Taussig dies in automobile accident

2001
First successful use of totally implantable artificial heart

Glossary

anatomy   the study of the structure of the body and its parts.

antivivisectionist   someone who opposes experimenting on animals, especially in ways that cause them pain or stress.

aorta   the main vessel that carries blood from the heart to the body.

arteries   the blood vessels that carry oxygen-rich blood from the heart through the body.

atria (singular atrium)   the upper two chambers of the heart, which receive blood from the body. Formerly called **auricles.**

Blalock-Taussig shunt   formal name for the procedure (popularly called the blue-baby operation), invented by Alfred Blalock, Helen Taussig, and Vivien Thomas in 1945, in which the subclavian artery is connected to the pulmonary artery in order to bypass a narrowed part of the latter artery (usually caused by a birth defect) and bring additional blood to the lungs.

blood type (blood group)   one of four major (and a number of minor) groups into which people are classified according to the kind of antigens (immune-triggering substances) that their red blood cells carry; receiving a transfusion from a person with a different blood type may cause an immune reaction that results in severe illness or death.

blue baby   popular term for a child with cyanosis. *See* **cyanosis.**

blue baby operation   popular term for the Blalock-Taussig shunt. *See* **Blalock-Taussig shunt.**

cardiac   pertaining to the heart.

cardiology   the medical specialty concerned with the heart.

cardiopulmonary resuscitation (CPR)   a technique for reviving people with stopped or fibrillating hearts, consisting chiefly of chest compressions, plus use of a defibrillator if available.

coarctation of the aorta   a birth defect that produces a narrowing of the aorta, resulting in dangerously high blood pressure in the arms and head.

congenital   existing at or before birth.

coronary artery   one of several arteries that carry the blood that nourishes the heart muscle.

crush syndrome   a form of delayed shock seen in people whose bodies have been partly crushed by heavy objects for long periods.

cyanosis   blueness of the skin, caused by too little oxygen in the blood.

cyclosporine   a drug, introduced in 1980, that prevents the immune system of an organ transplant recipient from attacking the donor organ.

defibrillator   a device that uses electricity to stop heart fibrillation. *See also* **fibrillation.**

ductus arteriosus   a short blood vessel (shunt) that connects the pulmonary artery to the aorta, bypassing the lungs, before birth; it normally closes at birth. *See also* **patent ductus arteriosus.**

dyslexia   a learning disability that causes trouble in learning to read, thought to be due to abnormalities in the brain.

endocrine disruptor   a substance that causes problems with health or reproduction by mimicking hormones or blocking their action. *See also* **hormone.**

fibrillation   a state in which the fibers of the heart muscle twitch randomly rather than contracting together in their normal, orderly pattern of beats; if not reversed immediately, it can cause death.

fluoroscope   a machine that uses X-rays passing through the body to create a glowing image of interior body parts (for example, the heart) on a screen.

heart-lung machine   popular term for oxygenator. *See* **oxygenator.**

hemoglobin   a pigment in red blood cells that carries oxygen and gives blood its color.

hormone   a substance produced by cells in one part of the body that influences the activity of cells in another part.

hypothermia   a condition in which the body's temperature drops significantly below normal; it has sometimes been deliberately induced to slow the heart and metabolism during surgery.

immune system   the system of cells and chemicals that defends the body against microorganisms and foreign substances.

intern   a young physician who has just completed medical school and earned an M.D. degree and is taking on-the-job training in a hospital.

open-heart surgery   surgery on the heart and nearby blood vessels in which the heart is stopped and the circulation is taken over by an oxygenator (heart-lung machine). *See also* **oxygenator.**

oxygenator   a device through which blood can be pumped during surgery; it adds oxygen to the blood (which is then returned to the body), temporarily taking over the functions of the heart and lungs and allowing the heart to be stopped.

patent ductus arteriosus   a ductus arteriosus that does not close after birth (a form of birth defect). *See also* **ductus arteriosus.**

pediatric cardiology   the medical subspecialty that treats children with heart ailments.

pediatrics   the medical specialty that treats children.

pericardium   the sacklike membrane that surrounds the heart.

phocomelia   a form of birth defect, popularly called "seal limbs," in which a child is born without arms (and sometimes legs), having instead flipperlike appendages attached directly to the body.

plasma   the liquid (cell-free) part of the blood.

protein   a member of a large class of natural substances that do most of the work in cells.

pulmonary artery   the vessel that carries blood from the right ventricle of the heart to the lungs.

pulmonary vein   the vessel that carries blood from the lungs to the left atrium of the heart.

resident   a physician undergoing the final stage of medical education, in which a doctor who has completed internship lives at a hospital and treats patients independently under the supervision of more experienced physicians.

rheumatic fever   a disease caused by streptococcus bacteria, which frequently damages the heart; it usually can be prevented or cured by antibiotics.

septum   the solid wall of muscle that separates the right chambers (atrium and ventricle) of the heart from the left chambers.

shock   a condition, resulting from loss of fluid in the blood, which can cause circulatory collapse and death if untreated.

stenosis   narrowing, for instance in a blood vessel.

strep throat   a sore throat caused by streptococcus bacteria; if untreated, it can be followed by rheumatic fever, a much more serious condition. *See also* **rheumatic fever.**

subclavian artery   the artery that carries blood to the head and arms (or forelegs in four-footed animals).

suture   to sew surgically; also, the thread used in such sewing.

tetralogy of Fallot   a group of four heart-related birth defects that usually occur together: narrowing of the pulmonary artery, enlarged right ventricle, hole in the heart septum, and abnormal position of the aorta that allows oxygen-poor blood to enter that vessel.

thalidomide   a drug used in the late 1950s to induce sleep and control nausea; it was found to cause severe birth defects if pregnant women took it.

transposition of the great vessels   a birth defect in which the points of origin of the aorta and the pulmonary artery are reversed; it is usually accompanied by a hole in the wall (septum) of the heart, allowing oxygenated and unoxygenated blood to mix.

tuberculosis   a disease caused by bacteria, which primarily attacks the lungs; it now can be treated by antibiotics but formerly was often fatal.

veins   the vessels that carry oxygen-depleted blood from the body to the heart.

ventricle   one of the two lower chambers of the heart.

Further Resources

Books

Baldwin, Joyce. *To Heal the Heart of a Child: Helen Taussig, M.D.* New York: Walker & Co., 1992.

 This book for young adults is the only book-length biography of Taussig. The author interviewed many of Taussig's colleagues and friends.

Blalock, Alfred. *Principles of Surgical Care: Shock and Other Problems.* St. Louis, Mo.: C. V. Mosby Company, 1940.

 Describes Blalock's pioneering conclusions about shock, including the basic cause and nature of this condition, types of shock, and treatments to prevent or halt shock.

"Blalock, Alfred; Taussig, Helen B(rooke)." In *Current Biography 1946.* New York: H. W. Wilson, 1946.

 Joint biographical sketch of Blalock and Taussig, published at the height of the blue baby operation's popularity. The article does not mention Vivien Thomas.

Harvey, A. McGehee. *Adventures in Medical Research: A Century of Discovery at Johns Hopkins.* Baltimore: Johns Hopkins University Press, 1974.

 Contains a chapter on Hopkins's role in cardiovascular research, which includes a discussion of the contributions of Alfred Blalock and some of the surgeons he trained.

Hurt, R. *The History of Cardiothoracic Surgery: From Early Times.* Oxford, England: Taylor & Francis, 1996.

 Presents the history of operations on the chest and heart, including the blue baby operation. Heart surgery was rare before the 1940s.

Longmire, William P., Jr. *Alfred Blalock: His Life and Times.* Baltimore: Privately printed, 1991.

Biography of Blalock by one of his former chief residents and a lifelong friend. It emphasizes Blalock's contributions at the expense of those of Taussig and Thomas.

Nuland, Sherwin B. *Doctors: The Biography of Medicine.* New York: Random House, 1988.
Contains a chapter on Helen Taussig and her role in developing the blue baby operation.

Ravitch, Mark M., ed. *A Century of Surgery: 1880–1980.* 2 vols. New York: Lippincott/Wiliams & Wilkins, 1981.
Summarizes papers presented at yearly meetings of the American Surgical Association during the years in question, as well as follow-up discussions. The papers include key presentations by Alfred Blalock, Robert Gross, and other pioneers of heart surgery.

———. *The Papers of Alfred Blalock.* 2 vols. Baltimore: The Johns Hopkins Press, 1966.
Includes an extensive biographical sketch of Blalock by Ravitch, one of Blalock's early chief residents and a lifelong friend and admirer, as well as all of Blalock's scientific papers.

Stoney, William S. *Pioneers of Cardiac Surgery.* Nashville, Tenn.: Vanderbilt University Press, 2008.
Contains autobiographical sketches by 38 members of the first two generations of heart surgeons, many of whom trained under Alfred Blalock and also knew Vivien Thomas. The book also includes a chronology and summary of the early years of cardiac surgery.

Taussig, Helen B. *Congenital Malformations of the Heart.* Revised edition; 2 vols. Cambridge, Mass.: Harvard University Press, 1960.
Taussig's classic textbook on birth defects that affect the heart and nearby blood vessels. The first volume discusses general considerations, especially methods of diagnosis, and the second volume describes particular defects, including the tetralogy of Fallot.

Thomas, Vivien T. *Pioneering Research in Surgical Shock and Cardiovascular Surgery.* Philadelphia: University of Pennsylvania Press, 1985.
Vivien Thomas's autobiography, describing his contributions to the blue baby operation and other surgical advances during the years he was Alfred Blalock's laboratory technician.

Watkins, Levi, Jr. "Vivien T. Thomas, LL.D. (Hon.): Instructor in Surgery, Johns Hopkins University." In Claude H. Organ, Jr., and Margaret M. Kosiba, eds. *A Century of Black Surgeons: The U.S.A. Experience.* Norman, Okla: Transcript Press, 1987, pp. 559–578.

A biographical sketch of Thomas by the first African-American cardiac chief resident at Johns Hopkins, who knew Thomas in Thomas's later years. The sketch is followed by reminiscences of Thomas by William P. Longmire, Jr., and Rowena Spencer.

Internet Resources

"Alfred Blalock." Who Named It? Available online. URL: http://www.whonamedit.com/doctor.cfm/2036.html. Accessed April 8, 2011.

Site presents a brief biography of Blalock, a description of the blue baby operation, and links to related pages on several surgical procedures named after Blalock. Includes mention of Vivien Thomas's role.

Aponte, Dulce. "Biography: Vivien Thomas." Helium.com. Available online. URL: http://www.helium.com/items/190785-biography-vivien-thomas. Accessed April 8, 2011.

Online article presents a brief biography of Thomas.

"The Blue Baby Operation." Alan Mason Chesney Medical Archives, Johns Hopkins Medical Institutions. 1995. Available online. URL: http://www.medicalarchives.jhmi.edu/page1.htm. Accessed April 8, 2011.

Site on the operation includes illustrated biographical sketches of Alfred Blalock, Helen Taussig, and Vivien Thomas.

"Cut to the Heart." Public Broadcasting System/WGBH (Boston). 1997. Available online. URL: http://www.pbs.org/wgbh/nova/heart. Accessed April 8, 2011.

This site was built to accompany a television program on heart surgery, part of the NOVA series, which was first broadcast on April 8, 1997. It includes sections on pioneers of heart surgery (chiefly development of open-heart surgery in the 1950s), treating a sick heart, and images of sick and healthy hearts.

"Dr. Helen Brooke Taussig." Changing the Face of Medicine: Celebrating America's Women Physicians (National Library of Medicine). Available online. URL: http://www.nlm.nih.gov/changingthefaceofmedicine/physicians/biography_316.html. Accessed April 8, 2011.

Brief biography of Helen Taussig, with photographs.

Moore, Francis D., and Judah Folkman. "Robert Edward Gross, July 2, 1905–October 11, 1988." Available online. URL: http://www.nap.edu/readingroom. php?book=biomems&page=rgross.html. Accessed April 8, 2011.

Biographical sketch of Robert Gross, who in 1938 became the first surgeon to repair a birth defect involving blood vessels close to the heart (patent, or open, ductus arteriosus).

"Partners of the Heart." Public Broadcasting System/WGBH (Boston). 2003. Available online. URL: http://www.pbs.org/wgbh/amex/partners/index. html. Accessed April 8, 2011.

Site for this television documentary, part of the American Experience series, features a transcript of the documentary, which focuses on Vivien Thomas's role in developing the blue baby operation and other surgical advances and his relationship with Alfred Blalock. The site also includes further reading, background on heart surgery and discrimination against African Americans, an interactive description of the operation, and questions for students and teachers.

"Vivien Thomas Fund." Johns Hopkins Medical Institutions. Available online. URL: http://www.hopkinsmedicine.org/stlm/vtfund.html. Accessed April 8, 2011.

Web page reviews Vivien Thomas's role in developing the historic blue baby operation at Hopkins and describes the Vivien Thomas Fund, established in his name to improve diversity at Hopkins.

Periodicals

Altman, Lawrence K. "Dr. Helen Taussig, 87, Dies; Led in Blue Baby Operation." *New York Times*, 22 May 1986.

Obituary article on Taussig reviews her accomplishments, featuring the blue baby operation.

Blalock, Alfred. "Experimental Shock: The Cause of the Low Blood Pressure Produced by Muscle Injury." *Archives of Surgery* 20 (June 1930): 959 ff.

Scientific article in which Blalock outlines his theory about the cause of shock and describes experiments on dogs that provide evidence for it.

———. "Mechanism and Treatment of Experimental Shock. I. Shock Following Hemorrhage." *Archives of Surgery* 15 (November 1927): 762 ff.

Blalock's first major scientific paper on shock, in which he describes the process by which shock develops in the body after blood loss and evaluates common treatments for shock.

————, and Helen B. Taussig. "The Surgical Treatment of Malformations of the Heart in Which There Is Pulmonary Stenosis or Pulmonary Atresia." *Journal of the American Medical Association* 128 (May 19, 1945): 189–202.
    Groundbreaking article in which Blalock and Taussig describe the first three blue baby operations.

Engle, Mary Allen. "Dr. Helen B. Taussig, the Tetralogy of Fallot, and the Growth of Pediatric Cardiac Services in the United States." *Johns Hopkins Medical Journal* 140 (April 1977): 147–150.
    Focuses on Taussig's role in developing the specialty of pediatric cardiology and training pediatric cardiologists.

Froslid, E. Kenneth. "Helen Taussig, M.D.—Savior of Blue Babies." *Today's Health* (August 1968): 48–51, 63–64.
    Biographical article on Taussig, written for a nonprofessional audience.

Harvey, A. McGehee. "Helen Brooke Taussig." *Johns Hopkins Medical Journal* 140 (April 1977): 137–141.
    Biographical article on Taussig includes background on Johns Hopkins Medical School's openness to women, the dispute about credit for the blue baby operation, and Taussig's role in revealing the dangers of thalidomide to unborn children in the early 1960s.

McCabe, Katie. "Like Something the Lord Made." *Washingtonian* (August 1989): 108–111, 226–233.
    This extensive article, which won a National Magazine Award, brought Vivien Thomas's contributions and career to public attention.

McGreevy, James M. "The Other Contributions of Alfred Blalock." *Current Surgery* 60 (March–April 2003): 160–163.
    This biographical article on Blalock stresses his contributions to medicine other than the blue baby operation, including his research on shock and his training of pioneer heart surgeons.

Merrill, Walter H. "What's Past Is Prologue." *Annals of Thoracic Surgery* 68 (1999): 2,366–2,375.
    Extensive biographical article on Alfred Blalock stresses people who influenced him, such as Barney Brooks and Tinsley Harrison. It includes a number of interesting quotations and other useful material.

Murphy, Anne M., and Duke E. Cameron. "The Blalock-Taussig-Thomas Collaboration: A Model for Medical Progress." *Journal of the American Medical Association* 300 (July 16, 2008): 328–330.

Reviews progress in treating children with heart defects and in redressing social injustices in medicine since Blalock and Taussig's milestone 1945 JAMA article about the blue baby operation. The article also show how the cooperation among Blalock, Taussig, and Vivien Thomas provided a model for cooperation across medical disciplines.

Neill, Catherine A. "Profiles in Pediatrics II: Helen Brooke Taussig." *Journal of Pediatrics* 125 (September 1994): 499–502.

Biographical sketch on Taussig includes material on her later life, such as her role in the thalidomide scandal.

Taussig, Helen B. "The Development of the Blalock-Taussig Operation and Its Results Twenty Years Later." *Proceedings of the American Philosophical Society* 120 (February 1976): 13–20.

Taussig reviews the development of the blue baby operation and the survival and progress of the children on which Alfred Blalock performed the surgery between 1945 and 1951. She reports that many went on to attend college, join the workforce, and raise families, showing that their brains had not been damaged by lack of oxygen in their early years.

———. "The Thalidomide Syndrome." *Scientific American* 207 (August 1962): 29–35.

In this article, Taussig describes in detail the epidemic of phocomelia (seal-limb) birth defects that resulted when pregnant women took thalidomide, a supposedly safe sleeping and anti-nausea medication.

Timmermans, Stefan. "A Black Technician and Blue Babies." *Social Studies of Science* 33 (April 2003): 197–229.

Timmermans describes Vivien Thomas's contributions to surgical research, his relationship with Alfred Blalock, and the "status dilemma" resulting from the conflict between expectations of Thomas as an African American and as a research professional.

Toledo-Pereyra, Luis H. "Alfred Blalock: Surgeon, Educator, and Pioneer in Shock and Cardiac Research." *Journal of Investigative Surgery* 18 (2005): 161–165.

Biographical article on Blalock discusses his contributions to medicine.

Index